BUILT to LAST

18th Century
FURNITURE

BUILT to LAST

18th Century
FURNITURE

skills institute press

Distributed By
Fox Chapel Publishing

FOX CHAPEL
PUBLISHING

18th Century Furniture is an original work, first published in 2011.

Portions of text and art previously published by and reproduced under license with Direct
Holdings Americas Inc.

ISBN: 978-1-56523-608-0

Library of Congress Cataloging-in-Publication Data

18th century furniture. -- 1st ed.
     p. cm. -- (Built to last)
 Includes index.
 Summary: "Woodworkers and furniture enthusiasts alike have long loved the practical, durable,
and attractive style of 18th century furniture, and this collection of projects are suitable to grace
all home interiors - from traditional layouts to more contemporary arrangements. A step-by-
step instruction aid, each project is accompanied by detailed shop drawings that break down
component parts into a manageable assemblage"-- Provided by publisher.
 ISBN 978-1-56523-608-0 (pbk.)
 1. Furniture making. I. Title: Eighteenth century furniture.
 TT194.C493 2011
 684.1'04--dc23
                              2011013303

To learn more about the other great books from Fox Chapel Publishing,
or to find a retailer near you, call toll-free 800-457-9112 or visit us at
www.FoxChapelPublishing.com.

Note to Authors: We are always looking for talented authors to write new books
in our area of woodworking, design, and related crafts. Please send a brief letter
describing your idea to Acquisition Editor, 1970 Broad Street, East Petersburg, PA 17520.

Printed in China
First printing

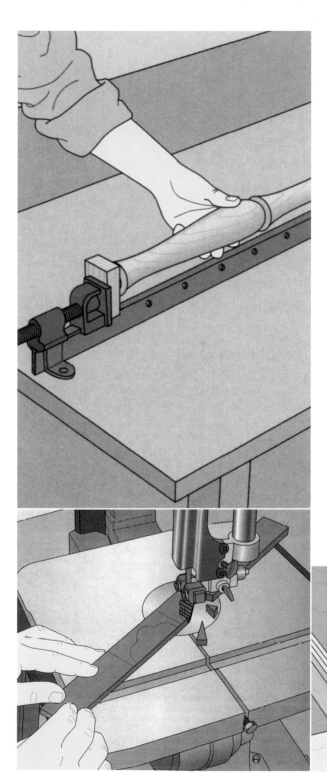

Contents

What You Can Learn

Cabinetmaking Basics, page 8

This chapter looks in detail at the basic skills you will need to select stock, prepare it, and then assemble it into a sturdy foundation for your project.

Jewelry Box, page 18

This jewelry box relies on traditional joinery techniques to transform a basic container into an attractive and useful treasury.

Shaker Candle Stand, page 25

Candle stands like the one in this chapter are light, stable, and easy to transport.

Blanket Chest, page 34

The blanket chest at the foot of a bed can store everything from toys to clothing to books, and performs double duty as a seating place.

Four-Poster Bed, page 56

This project takes the dramatic four-poster bed and makes it manageable to build and assemble.

Queen Anne Secretary, page 78

The Queen Anne secretary desk in this chapter is more elegant that those of the 17th Century, but less ornate than some later examples.

Philadelphia-style Highboy, page 114

This chapter will show you how to design and construct a classic highboy.

Pembroke Table, page 148

This Pembroke table was built to require as little space as possible while still being ultra functional.

CHAPTER 1:
CABINETMAKING BASICS

There are two kinds of skill involved in constructing a fine cabinet or bookcase: putting together the basic skeleton of the piece and then embellishing it. The finials and rosettes of the Queen Anne highboy featured on page 78 must be turned with care on a lathe and then artfully carved; the distinctive pilasters of an armoire require careful attention to produce on the router. But although these distinctive adornments may capture a viewer's attention, they also reflect a truism: No amount of decoration will conceal the defects of a poorly built structure. This chapter looks in detail at the basic skills you will need to select stock, prepare it professionally, and then assemble it into a sturdy foundation for your cabinet or bookcase.

The basics of cabinetmaking begin with an understanding of wood. The sections on dealing with wood movement *(page 9)*, ordering wood *(page 11)*, and preparing

a cutting list based on a sketch *(page 13)* will help you purchase the right lumber for your project.

With your stock in hand, you can begin the step-by-step process of building a carcase.

The frame-and-panel method of building a door is described starting on page 109. This technique is popular not only for its appearance, but because it allows for wood movement. In many frame-and-panel cabinets, the panels are "raised"—that is, they have bevels cut around their edges. Not only do the bevels lend a decorative touch, but they also allow the wood to expand and contract while preserving the work's integrity.

Panels are often made of boards edge-glued together. The pieces should produce a pattern that is visually interesting, while the grain of all the boards should run in the same direction. A marked triangle will help you rearrange the boards correctly if they are moved before glue up.

Wood Movement

Wood is a hygroscopic material, absorbing and releasing moisture as the relative humidity of the surrounding air rises and falls. And as the moisture content of a piece of wood changes, so do its dimensions and weight. When wood is assembled into a piece of furniture, the changes can produce problems—some great, some small. A cabinet door that shuts smoothly in December may not close at all in June; a perfectly square bookcase can literally pull itself apart at the joints as humidity changes throughout the year.

The water in wood is measured as a percentage of its oven-dry, or water-free weight. For example, if a 40-pound piece of wood drops to 30 pounds when oven-dried, the weight of the shed water—10 pounds—divided by the wood's dry weight—30 pounds—is the moisture content of the original piece: in this case, 33 percent.

Wood holds water both as vapor-like moisture called free water in its cell cavities and as bound water in the cell walls. When wood is cut and exposed to the air, it sheds its free water first. When all free water is expelled, the wood is said to be at its fiber saturation point (FSP), typically between 23 and 30 percent moisture content.

Under normal circumstances, wood never regains its free water; a dried board's cell cavities will always remain empty of moisture. But the amount of bound water contained in the cell walls changes with shifts in the humidity in the air. At 100 percent relative humidity, wood reaches its FSP. At 0 percent humidity, wood is drained of all water. The relative moisture in the atmosphere

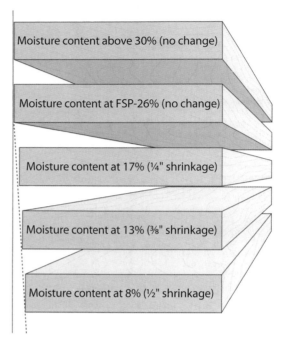

As the moisture level of a 2-by-10 plain-sawn plank of softwood lumber drops below the fiber saturation point (FSP), the wood shrinks. At 17 percent, the board is ¼ inch narrower than it was at its FSP; it loses another ¼ inch of width when kiln-dried to 8 percent. Shrinkage depends partly on the density of the wood; generally, a denser species shrinks and swells more than a lighter one. Sapwood also tends to change in size more quickly than heartwood.

normally falls between these values, and the moisture content of most woods ranges between 5 and 20 percent.

You can compensate for this in several ways. Use a humidifier in winter and a dehumidifier in summer to keep the indoor level of humidity as constant as possible. Remember to make allowances for wood movement in the construction of your work. Consult a lumber dealer to find the most dimensionally stable species for your projects.

Wood Shrinkage

Tangential and radial shrinkage. Wood does not shrink uniformly; as shown by the dotted red lines in the illustration at right, tangential shrinkage—tangent to the growth rings—is about twice as great as radial shrinkage, which occurs across the rings. This difference causes boards and panels to warp as they shrink or swell with changes in relative humidity. It can also cause joints to loosen or tighten from excess pressure, as discussed below. Shrinkage along the length of a board is usually insignificant. A 2-by-10 plank that shrinks ½ inch across its width might lose less than 1/16 inch along an 8-foot length.

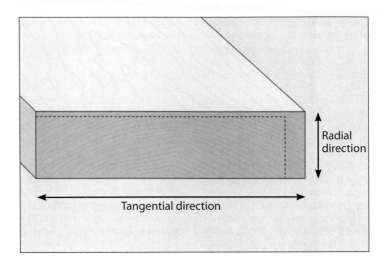

Radial direction

Tangential direction

Wood Grain and Joinery

Optimizing grain direction. The location of the tangential planes of mating boards will significantly affect a joint's strength and stability. In the ideal situation—as shown in the illustration of a mortise-and-tenon joint at right—the tangential planes of joined pieces are parallel. This ensures that the boards will experience similar wood movement in the same direction as their moisture content changes. Orienting boards this way helps prevent a joint from coming loose; it also prevents the mating boards from splitting when they swell with higher levels of moisture.

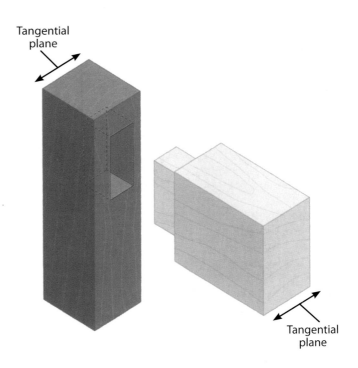

Tangential plane

Tangential plane

Selecting and Ordering Lumber

You can buy the lumber for your woodworking project from several sources, each with its own advantages and drawbacks. The local lumberyard is often the most convenient supplier, but the selection may be limited to construction woods such as pine, spruce, and other softwoods. Though you may find the occasional cache of hardwood at a lumberyard, you will probably have to venture further afield, consulting woodworking magazines to find dealers who specialize in the hardwoods used in cabinetry. Prices for good hardwood lumber can be high, but as is often the case, you will generally get what you pay for.

Sometimes you can buy locally cut lumber from a small sawmill, but the wood will often need to be seasoned and surfaced. Recycled boards are growing in popularity, a result of the scarcity of certain woods and the growing sense

Calculating Board Feet

Ordering lumber by the board foot

The board foot is a unit of measurement commonly used when dealing with hardwood lumber. As shown below, the standard board foot is equivalent to a piece of wood 1 inch thick, 12 inches wide, and 12 inches long. To calculate the number of board feet in a particular piece of wood, multiply its three dimensions, then divide the result by 144 if the dimensions are all in inches, or by 12 if one of the dimensions is in feet.

**Number of board feet
in eight lineal feet of
different size boards**

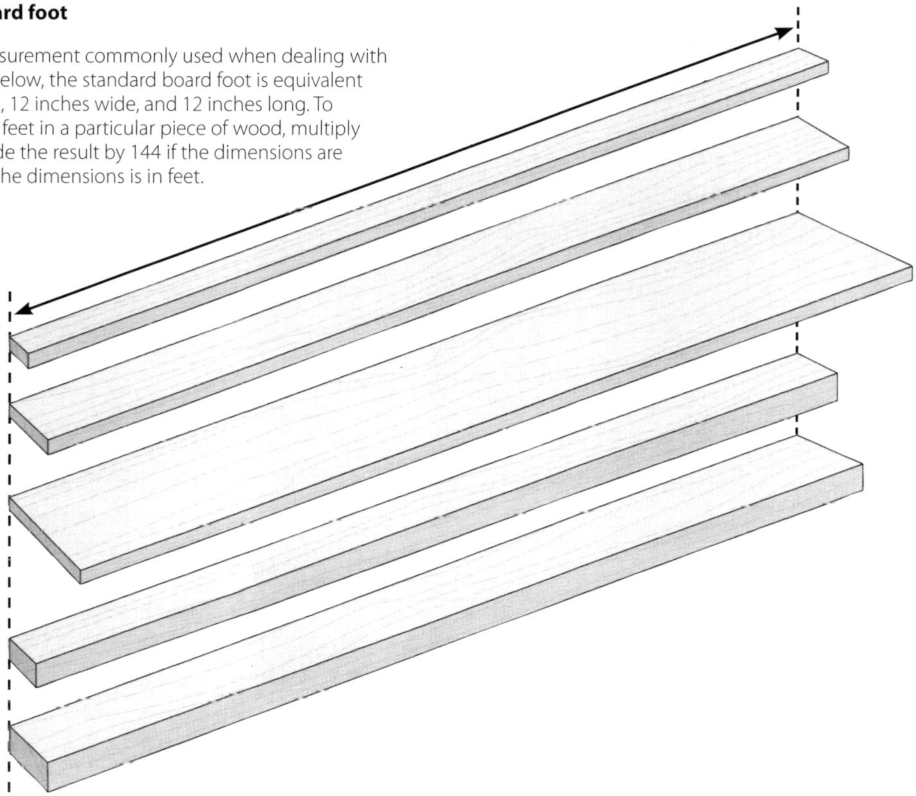

1-by-3 = 2 board feet

1-by-6 = 4 board feet

1-by-12 = 8 board feet

2-by-4 = 5⅓ board feet

2-by 6 = 8 board feet

1" x 12" x 12" = 1 standard board foot

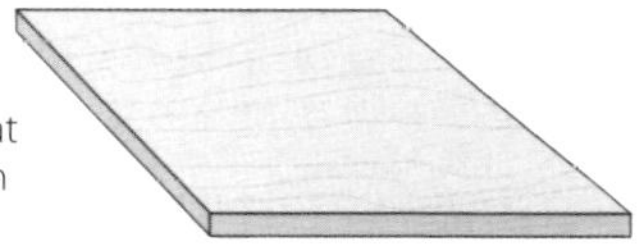

The formula for a standard board foot:
1" × 12" × 12" ÷ 144 = 1 (or 1" × 12" × 1' ÷ 12 = 1)
So if you had a 6-foot-long 1-by-4, you would calculate the board feet as follows: 1" × 4" × 6' ÷ 12 = 2 (or 2 board feet). Other examples are shown in the illustration. Remember that board feet are calculated on the basis of nominal rather than actual dimensions.

of environmental responsibility felt by many woodworkers. Whether removed from an old barn or a piece of timeworn furniture, such wood may be relatively inexpensive and, because it often originates from old growth timber, it can be visually and structurally superior to the small billets of younger lumber available today.

Before ordering your wood, consider your requirements carefully and refer to the following tips to help you get what you need at a reasonable cost.

• **Species:** Ask for the specific wood species, not a broad family name. For example, order Western red cedar, not simply cedar. To be absolutely sure, learn the botanical name of the wood you want and ask for it.

• **Quantity:** Let your supplier know whether you are ordering in board feet or lineal feet. A lineal foot refers to a board's length, regardless of its width and thickness. The board foot is a measure of the volume of wood; it is usually necessary to refer to board feet for ordering hardwoods, which are often available in random sizes only.

• **Size:** Wood is sold in nominal rather than actual sizes, so make allowances for the difference when ordering surfaced lumber. A nominal 2-by-4 is actually 1½"-by-3½". The thickness of wood is often expressed as a fraction in quarters of an inch. A 2-inch-thick board, for example, is expressed as 8/4; surfacing will reduce it to 1¾ inches. With unsurfaced or green wood, the nominal and actual dimensions are the same.

• **Grade:** The primary difference between high and low grades of hardwood lumber is appearance rather than strength. Because the grade of a board is determined by the proportions of clear wood it contains, large high-grade boards are far more expensive than lower-grade boards. If you need only smaller high-grade pieces you can cut them out of a lower-grade board, at great savings. Consult your local dealer for a chart of the different grades available.

• **Seasoning:** Lumber is sold either kiln-dried (KD) or air-dried (AD). The primary difference between the two is the moisture content (MC) of the wood. Kiln-dried wood has a moisture content of about 8 percent; it will not dry any further when used for indoor furniture. Air-dried wood has an MC of 12 to 15 percent. This wood is often chosen by carvers, or by woodworkers who prefer to dry their own wood.

• **Surfacing:** Surfacing refers to how wood is prepared at the mill before it comes to the lumberyard. Hardwood lumber is usually surfaced on both faces (S2S). If you have a planer and a jointer, buying rough lumber and surfacing it yourself will prove less expensive.

The Stages of Cabinet Production

Like most tasks, the building of a piece of furniture can be accomplished most smoothly and efficiently if you take a methodical approach. Most projects involve the steps listed below; they should be carried out in the sequence shown, starting at the drawing board and ending with a final inspection. For maximum efficiency, lay out your tools in the shop so that your wood follows a relatively direct route from rough stock to final assembly. Considerations for determining your needs and ordering wood are discussed above. Stock preparation begins on page 15.

- Design and plan piece
- List and order materials
- Prepare stock
- Joint one face and edge
- Plane other face
- Rip to width
- Crosscut to length
- Cut joints
- Sand before assembly
- Assemble components
- Finish sand
- Make and install doors and drawers
- Apply finish
- Give final inspection

Cutting Lists

Making and using a cutting list. A cutting list records the finished sizes of lumber needed for a particular piece of furniture. If one is not included with the plans you purchase, you will have to make your own based on a sketch of the design. Use the formula shown on page 11 to total the number of board feet for each component of the project; add 20 to 40 percent (depending on the species) to account for waste and defects in the wood. For the bookcase shown at right, which totals roughly 14 board feet, you should purchase 17 to 20 board feet of 4/4 lumber in addition to the plywood for the back of the case. As shown below, a cutting list should include the name of the component, the quantity, the dimensions of each piece, and the wood species selected for the project. For convenience, assign each piece a key letter for later reference.

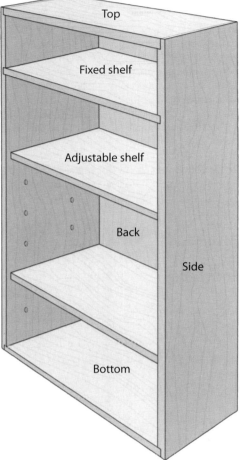

Cutting List

Piece	Quantity	Thickness	Width	Length	Material	Board feet
A Top	1	1"	10"	23¼"	ash	1.6
B Bottom	1	1"	10"	23¼"	ash	1.6
C Side	2	1"	10"	42"	ash	5.8
D Fixed shelf	1	1"	10"	23¼"	ash	1.6
E Adjustable shelves	2	1"	10"	22⅜"	ash	3.0
F Back	1	¼"	24"	42"	plywood	–

Lumber Defects

Lumber defects may reduce a board's strength or workability or mar its appearance. Or, in the hands of a creative woodworker, some defects may become visual assets, transforming an ordinary piece into a work of art.

The chart below illustrates some of the most common defects and details the way in which most can be corrected; with diligent use of the band saw, even the most seriously cupped boards can be salvaged *(page 16)*.

Defects in Wood

Type	Characteristics	Remedies
Knot	Appears as a whorl encircled by sound tissue. Live branches integrate with surrounding wood, resulting in tight knots; dead stubs cannot integrate with surrounding tissue, forming dead or loose knots.	Tight knots can be cut out or used, as appearance dictates; dead or loose knots must be removed before working with stock.
Gum	An accumulation on the surface of the board or in pockets within the board. Usually develops when a tree has suffered an injury, exposure to fire, or insect attack.	Do not use stock if a quality finish is required, as gum will bleed through most finishes.
Checks	Lengthwise ruptures or separations in the wood, usually caused by rapid drying. May compromise strength and appearance.	Can be cut off.
Bow	An end-to-end curve along the face, usually caused by improper storage of lumber. Makes it difficult to cut.	Flatten bowed boards on the jointer, or cut into shorter pieces, then use the jointer.
Cup	An edge-to-edge curve across the face. Common in tangentially cut stock, or boards cut close to the pith, if one face of a board has less contact with the air than the other.	Cupped boards can be salvaged on the band saw *(page 16)* or flattened on the jointer.
Crook	End-to-end curve along the edge, caused by incorrect seasoning or cutting the board close to the pith of a tree. Weakens the wood.	Board can be salvaged by jointing and ripping waste from the edges. Crooked boards remain unstable, and may not stain or finish well.
Twist	Uneven or irregular warping when one corner is not aligned with the others. Results from uneven drying or a cross-grain pattern that is not parallel to the edge.	Board can be flattened on jointer, or cut into shorter boards.
Split	Similar to checks, appearing as separations along the growth rings. Results from improper drying of wood or felling damage.	Board can be used, but split may mar the appearance of the wood, becoming more noticeable when stain is applied.

Preparing Stock

Once you have designed a project and purchased the lumber, you must prepare the stock, jointing and planing it smooth and square, cutting it to the proper dimensions and sanding any surfaces.

For rough, unsurfaced lumber, first smooth one face on the jointer, then one edge, producing two adjoining surfaces that are at 90° to each other. Next, plane the other face of the board to make it parallel to the first. When the stock is square and smooth, you are ready to rip it to width and crosscut it to length.

For S2S lumber, which has already had both faces surfaced, you need only joint one edge across the jointer, then cut to width and length. S4S stock,

A jointer produces a smooth, even edge on a hardwood board. For best results, set a cutting depth between $1/16$ and $1/8$ inch.

with all four surfaces dressed, can be ripped and crosscut immediately; only surfaces that will be glued together must be jointed. Before gluing, remember to sand any surfaces that will be hard to reach after assembly.

Surfacing Lumber

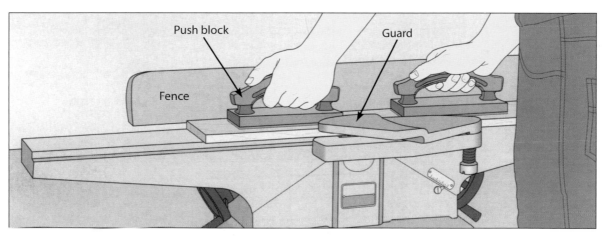

Push block

Guard

Fence

Jointing a board. Slide the fence toward the guard, if necessary, to ensure that no portion of the cutter knives will be exposed as the workpiece passes over them. Lay the workpiece face-down on the infeed table a few inches from the knives. Butt its edge against the fence, then place two push blocks squarely on its face, centered between the edges. (Use push blocks with offset handles to prevent your hands from hitting the fence.) Feed the board slowly and steadily across the knives *(above)* applying downward pressure on the outfeed side of the knives and lateral pressure against the fence. When working with long stock, bring your left hand to the back of the workpiece when your right hand passes the knives.

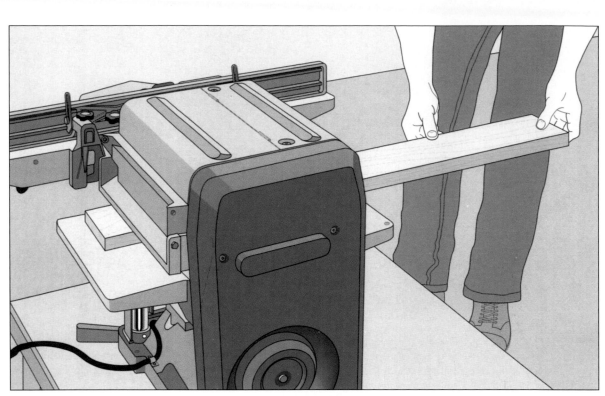

Planing stock. Set the cutting depth to ¹⁄₁₆ inch. Stand to one side of the planer and use both hands to feed the stock carefully into the machine. Once the feed mechanism grips the board and begins to pull it across the cutterhead, support the trailing end to keep it flat on the table *(above)*. Then move to the outfeed side of the planer to support the workpiece with both hands until it clears the outfeed roller. To prevent the stock from warping in use, avoid planing only one face; instead, plane the same amount of wood from both sides.

Shop Tip

Salvaging cupped stock on the band saw
You can salvage cupped boards using the band saw, radial arm saw, or table saw by ripping the stock into narrower boards. If you are using the band saw as shown here, install your widest blade and a rip fence. The narrower the width of cut, the flatter the resulting boards. Set the board convex (high) side up on the table and, butting the board against the fence, feed it steadily into the blade. Finish the pass with a push stick. Remove any remaining high spots on the jointer.

Dimensioning Stock

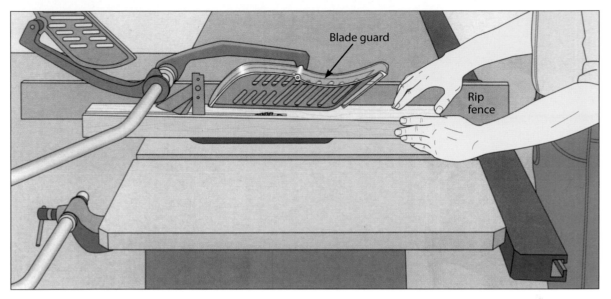

Blade guard

Rip fence

Ripping a board on the table saw. Set the blade height about ¼ inch above the workpiece. Position the rip fence for the width of cut, then push the stock into the blade, holding it firmly against the fence with your left hand and feeding the board with both thumbs *(above)*. Stand slightly to one side of the workpiece and straddle the fence with your right hand, making certain that neither hand is in line with the blade. Keep pushing the board until the blade cuts through it completely. To keep your fingers from coming closer than 3 inches from the blade, use a push stick to complete the pass. (**Caution: Blade guard partially retracted for clarity.**)

Crosscutting stock. With the workpiece flush against the miter gauge, align the cutting mark with the blade. Position the rip fence well away from the end of the stock to prevent the cut-off piece from jamming against the blade and kicking back toward you. Hook the thumbs of both hands over the miter gauge to hold the stock firmly against the gauge and flat on the table, then feed the board into the blade *(right)*. (**Caution: Blade guard partially retracted for clarity.**)

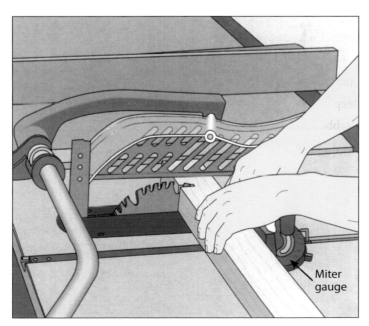

Miter gauge

CHAPTER 2

JEWELRY BOX

A jewelry box should do more than keep the dust off valuables. It should also suggest strength and security—and express the elegance of its contents. The box shown in the photo at left satisfies these requirements in a number of ways. It is made from an exotic hardwood—pau ferro—and is joined at the corners by through dovetails, a sturdy joint that adds visual interest. The half-mortise lock protects the contents from prying fingers and accents the design of the piece. The tray inside the box features dividers for sorting smaller items and is assembled with finger joints.

The jewelry box shown at right measures 9½ inches long by 6¼ inches deep and 5½ inches high. The box sits in a rabbeted base joined at the corners by miters. For a box of the proportions shown, use ½- to ⅝-inch-thick stock for the the box and ¼-inch-thick wood for the tray. To protect the jewelry from scratches, you can line the inside of the box and tray with a soft material such as felt or flocking.

Made from pau ferro, the jewelry box shown above measures 9½ inches long by 6¼ inches deep and 5½ inches high. The box sits in a rabbeted base joined at the corners by miters.

Making the Box

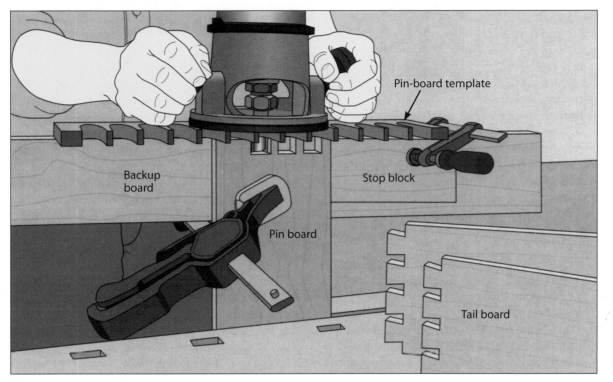

Pin-board template

Backup board

Stop block

Pin board

Tail board

1 **Routing the dovetails.** To cut the dovetails for the box with a router and the jig shown above, screw the pin- and tail-board templates to backup boards, then secure one of the tail boards (the sides of the box) end up in a bench vise. Clamp the tail template to the workpiece so the underside of the template is butted against the end of the board. Also clamp a stop block against one edge of the workpiece so the tails at the other end and in the other tail board will match. Install a top-piloted dovetail bit in the router and cut the tails

by feeding the tool along the top of the template and moving the bit in and out of the jig's slots. Keep the bit pilot pressed against the sides of the slots throughout. Repeat to rout the tails at the other end of the board, and in the other tail board. Then use the completed tails to outline the pins on the front and back of the box. Secure the pin board in the vise, clamp the pin template to the board with the slots aligned over the outline, and secure a stop block in place. Rout the pins with a straight bit *(above)*.

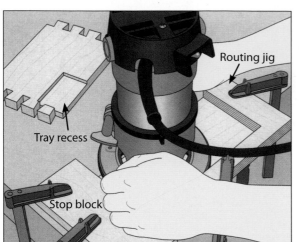

Tray recess

Routing jig

Stop block

2 **Routing the recesses for the tray.** The tray inside the box rests in a recess routed into both sides of the box. Before cutting the recesses, dry-assemble the box and determine what should be the top of the box depending on the grain and figure of the wood. Label the pieces to facilitate reassembly, then outline the recesses on the sides and set one of the pieces inside-face up on a work surface. You can make a simple jig to keep the router bit within the outline by cutting a notch out of a piece of plywood and clamping it to the workpiece. Also clamp a stop block along the tails to prevent from cutting into them. Install a straight bit in the router, set the cutting depth to ¼ inch and rout the recess. Repeat for the other side *(left)*, then square the corners with a chisel.

3 **Preparing the box for the bottom.** The bottom of the jewelery box fits into a rabbet along the inside of the box. Dry-fit the parts together, then clamp the unit securely, installing the jaws on the sides of the box. Fit a router with a piloted rabbeting bit of a diameter equal to one-half the thickness of the stock. Then mount the router in a table and set the cutting height to the thickness of the bottom panel you will be using. Set the box right-side up on the table and, starting at the middle of one side, feed the stock into the bit against the direction of bit rotation. Keeping the pilot bearing butted against the workpiece, feed the box clockwise *(right)*. Continue pivoting the box on the table until you return to your starting point. Use veneered plywood for the bottom and cut the panel to fit the opening. The plywood will not expand or contract with changes in humidity, allowing you to glue and nail it in place.

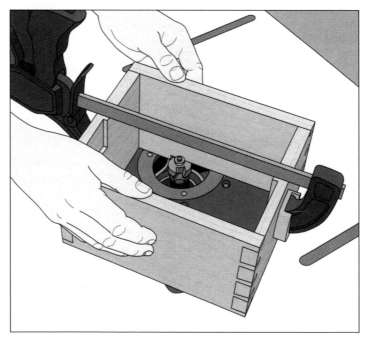

Installing the Lock

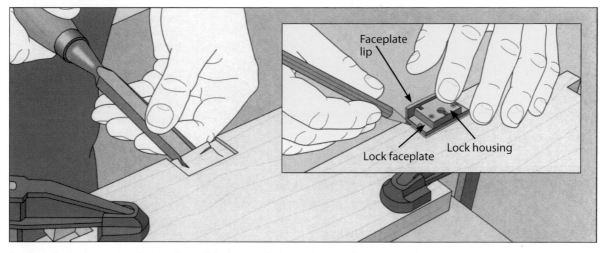

Faceplate lip

Lock housing

Lock faceplate

Cutting the lock mortise. Lay the front of the box inside-face up and position the lock face-down midway between the pins and flush with the top edge of the board. Trace the outline of the hardware *(inset)*, then extend the lines onto the top edge of the board. Now clamp the front of the box to your work surface and use a chisel to cut a shallow mortise for the faceplate lip in the top edge of the board. Score the mortise outline on the inside face of the board then, holding the chisel horizontally and bevel up, shave away the waste in thin layers *(above)*. The central portion of the mortise, which will hold the lock housing, must be deeper than the portion housing the faceplate.

Periodically test-fit the lock in the cavity and use the chisel to deepen or widen the mortise as necessary. Once the faceplate is flush with the inside face of the board, set the lock in the mortise and mark the location of the keyhole. (The mortise for the lock can also be cut out with a router, but work carefully, especially if you are doing the job freehand. Do not try to rout right to the edge of the mortise outline; instead, finish the cut with a chisel.) Now drill a hole for the key through the board and use a small, round file to refine the opening to the shape of the key, then install the escutcheon over the keyhole and screw the lock to the front of the box. You can now glue up the box.

Making the Base Molding

1 Shaping the molding stock.
Because the pieces for the base molding are relatively narrow, shape both edges of a wide board, then rip the molding from the board. Install a molding bit in a router and mount the tool in a table. To prevent kickback, use three featherboards, clamping one to the table in line with the bit and two to the fence, one on each side of the cutter. (The featherboard on the outfeed side of the fence has been removed for clarity.) Shape both edges of the board, feeding it along the fence *(right)*.

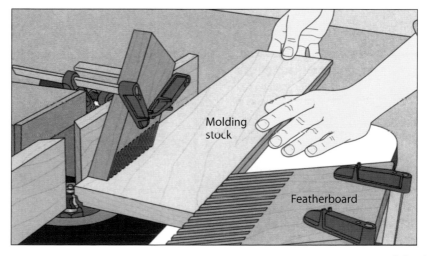

Molding stock

Featherboard

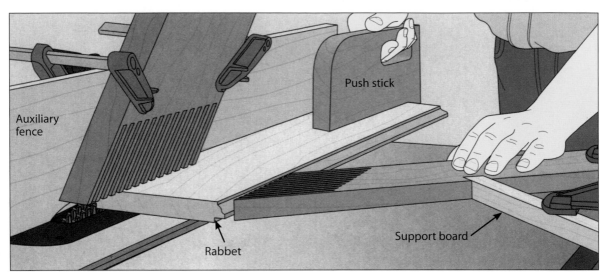

Auxiliary fence

Push stick

Rabbet

Support board

2 **Preparing the molding for the box.** Cut rabbets in the molding by fitting your table saw with a dado head. Adjust the width of the head to two-thirds the thickness of the stock and the cutting height to one-third the stock thickness. Fasten an auxiliary fence to the rip fence and notch it with the dado head. Use two featherboards to support the stock, clamping one to the fence above the blade and one to the

table; brace the second featherboard with a support board. Feed the stock along the fence to cut a rabbet on one edge, then repeat on the other edge, making both passes with a push stick *(above)*. Now rip the molding pieces from the board. If you wish, you can use a band saw to cut a relief pattern in the molding like the one shown in the photo on page 18, creating feet at each corner.

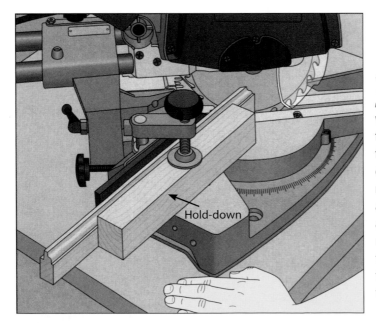

Hold-down

3 **Mitering and installing the molding.** You can saw the molding pieces to length with a miter box or on a power miter saw adjusted for a 45° cut. Lay the stock on edge against the fence, butt a board against the workpiece, and clamp it in place as a hold-down. To ensure the molding fits the box perfectly, make the first cuts a little long, test-fit the molding under the box, and trim the pieces to fit *(left)*. Spread glue on the mitered ends of the molding and secure the pieces together with a web clamp, using the box as a form. Once the glue has cured, apply adhesive in the rabbets and set the box on the molding.

Mounting the Lid

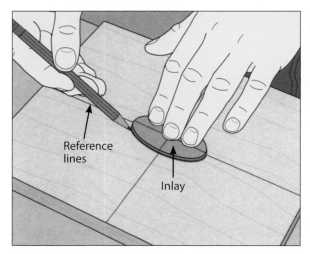

Reference lines

Inlay

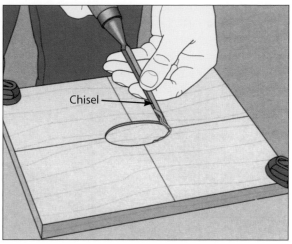

Chisel

1 **Installing the inlay.** Mark two lines across the lid of the box that intersect at its center. Mark corresponding lines that cross at the center of the inlay, then position the inlay on the top so the four reference marks line up and trace the outline with a pencil *(above, left)*. Clamp the top to a work surface and use a router fitted with a straight bit to cut the recess to within $\frac{1}{16}$ inch of your outline; the depth of the recess should equal the inlay thickness. To complete the recess, score the outline with a utility knife and cut to the marked outline with a chisel *(above, right)*. Then spread a thin coating of glue in the recess, set the inlay in place, and clamp it down using a wood block to distribute the pressure. Once the glue has cured, sand the inlay flush with the surface. Now install a piloted round-over bit in a router and bullnose the edges of the top by making a pass on each side, making sure you keep the bearing butted against the stock while you feed against the direction of bit rotation.

2 **Installing the lid hinges.** Attach the hinges to the jewelry box in two steps. Start by outlining one leaf of each hinge on the lid, then cut mortises within the outlines and fasten the hinges to the lid. Make the mortises $\frac{1}{32}$ inch deeper than the leaf thickness. Next, position the lid on the box and outline the remaining leaves on the top edge of the back of the box. Clamp the box to a work surface and use a chisel to cut the mortises *(right)*.

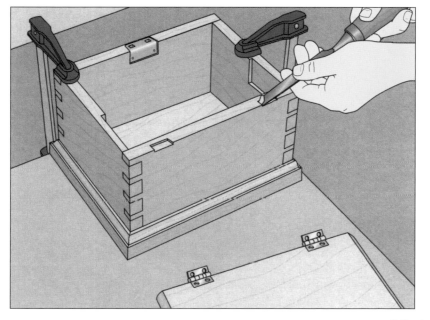

3 **Installing the lid and the lock strike plate.** Before fastening the hinges to the box, mount the strike plate to the underside of the lid. Position the plate on the lock and turn the key to hold the plate in place. Apply double-sided tape to the strike plate and position the lid on the box. Turn the key again to release the strike plate and remove the lid; the plate will be in position on the lid. Outline the strike plate on the surface, remove the tape, and cut a mortise within the outline to the depth of the plate. Then drill pilot holes and screw the plate in place *(right)*. To complete the lid installation, screw the hinges to the box.

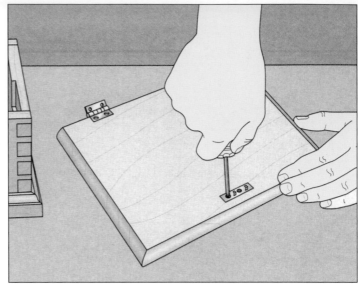

Installing the Tray

Making the tray. Cut the sides of the tray to fit in the recess in the box and join the pieces with box joints *(page 20)*. Before assembling the tray, cut dadoes for the dividers in the inside faces of the front and back. Glue up the tray, cut and insert the dividers *(left)*, and set the tray in the box. Sand the tray as necessary to fine-tune its fit. As a final touch, you can attach a chain to the lid and box to prevent the lid from opening too far and straining the hinges.

CHAPTER 3:
SHAKER CANDLE STAND

In an era before electricity, the Shakers depended on candles to see them though the hours of darkness. These diligent workers could not allow late sunrises or early dusks to interfere with their labor. Candle stands were light, stable, and easy to transport. Although candle stands were not a Shaker invention, the furniture makers in their communities elevated this commonplace item to its most refined expression.

The elegance of the candle stand's tripod design sacrifices some strength. Because of the angle at which they splay out, the legs are subjected to a great deal of racking stress which pulls them away from the column. The Shakers compensated for this weakness in several ways. The most important was attaching the legs to the column with sliding dovetails—very strong and durable joints. Some Shaker candle stands have survived 150 years and are as sturdy as the day they were made.

To give the legs added strength, a metal plate, known as a "spider," is nailed to the base of the column and legs. The design of the legs also fortifies the stand. They are ⅜ inch thicker at the top, which makes the dovetails that much stronger. Also, the Shakers cut the legs so the grain runs along their length, helping them resist stress.

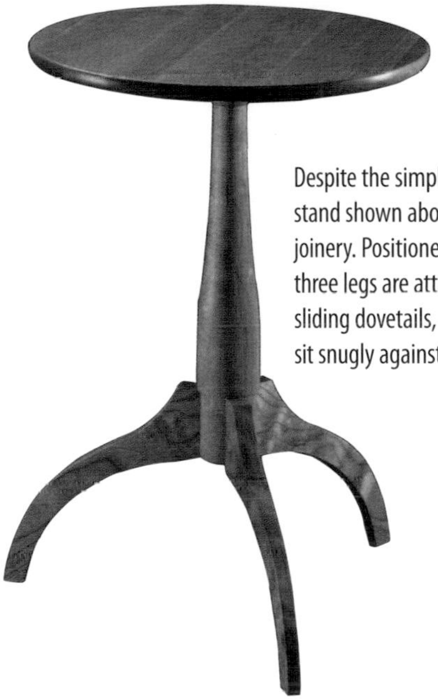

Despite the simple appearance of the candle stand shown above, the table relies on precise joinery. Positioned exactly 120° apart, the three legs are attached to the column with sliding dovetails, cut with angled shoulders to sit snugly against the column.

Anatomy of a Shaker Candle Stand

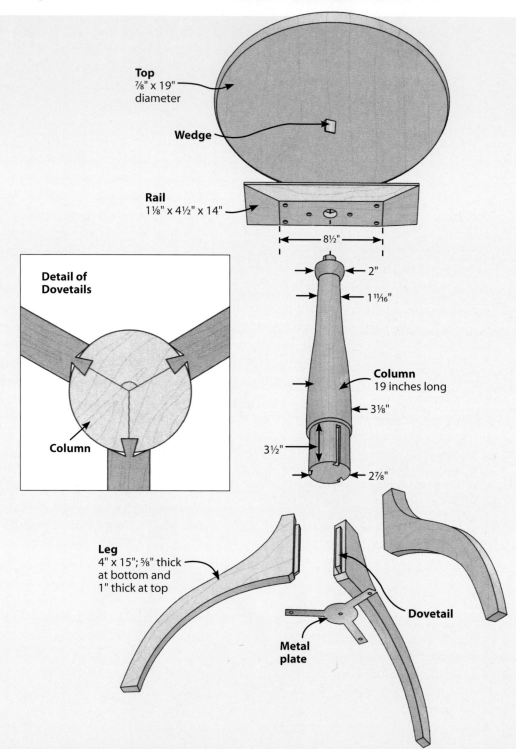

Top
⅞" x 19"
diameter

Wedge

Rail
1⅛" x 4½" x 14"

8½"

**Detail of
Dovetails**

Column

2"

1¹¹⁄₁₆"

Column
19 inches long

3⅛"

3½"

2⅞"

Leg
4" x 15"; ⅝" thick
at bottom and
1" thick at top

Dovetail

**Metal
plate**

Circle-Cutting Jig

To cut the circular top of a candle stand on your band saw, use the shop-built circle-cutting jig shown at right. Refer to the illustration for suggested dimensions.

Rout a ⅜-inch-deep dovetail channel in the middle of the jig base, then use a table saw to rip a thin board with a bevel along both edges to produce a bar that slides smoothly in the channel. (Set the saw blade angle by measuring the angle of the channel edges.) Cut out the notch on the band saw, then screw the support arms to the underside of the jig base, spacing them to hug the sides of the band saw table when the jig is in position. Drill two holes through the bottom of the dovetail channel in the jig base, 1 inch and 3 inches from the unnotched end; also bore two holes through the bar as shown.

To prepare the workpiece, mark the circumference and center of the circle on its underside. Then use the band saw to cut off the four corners of the panel to keep it from hitting the clamps that secure the jig. Next, make a release cut from the edge of the panel to the marked circumference, then veer off to the edge. Screw the pivot bar to the center of

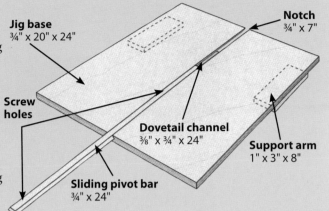

Jig base
¾" x 20" x 24"

Screw holes

Notch
¾" x 7"

Dovetail channel
⅜" x ¾" x 24"

Support arm
1" x 3" x 8"

Sliding pivot bar
¾" x 24"

the workpiece through one of the bar's holes, leaving the screw loose enough to pivot the panel.

Turn the workpiece over and mark the point where the blade contacted the circumference during the release cut. Clamp the jig base to the band saw table, making sure the support arms are butted against the table's edges. Slide the pivot bar into the channel in the base and pivot the panel until the marked contact point touches the blade. Screw through one of the holes in the jig base to lock the pivot bar in place *(below, left)*. Turn on the saw and pivot the workpiece into the blade in a clock-wise direction *(below, right)*, feeding the piece until the cut is completed.

Contact point

Circle circumference

Preparing the Top and Rail

1 Preparing the top. Once the top of the candle stand has been cut *(page 27)*, shape its circumference on a router table in two steps. Start by installing a piloted ½-inch radius bit in a router and mounting the tool in a table. Align the fence with the bit's pilot bearing and clamp a featherboard to the fence to support the top during the cut. Holding the top face-up and flat on the table, press the edge against the fence and rotate the stock into the bit *(right)*. Continue pivoting the top until the entire circumference is shaped, then switch to a piloted ¼-inch radius bit, turn the workpiece over, and repeat to shape its top side.

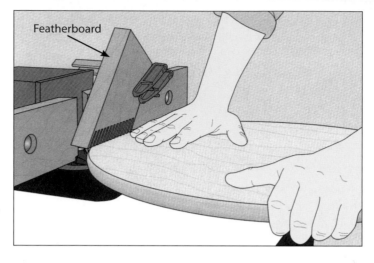

Featherboard

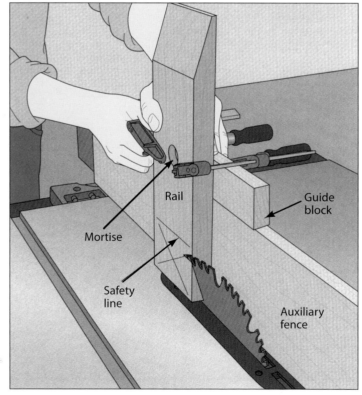

Rail

Mortise

Safety line

Guide block

Auxiliary fence

2 Making the rail. Referring to the anatomy illustration on page 140, cut the rail that will connect the column to the tabletop, then bore a mortise in the center of the rail to accept the tenon you will turn at the top of the column; a 1-inch-diameter hole is typical. Bevel the ends and edges of the rail on your table saw. Attach an auxiliary fence and position the fence to the left of the blade for a ¼-inch cutting width. Raise the blade to its maximum setting, adjust the angle to about 75°, and clamp a guide block to the rail to ride along the top of the fence. Mark a line across the face of the rail slightly above the height of the blade as a reminder to keep your hands well above the blade. Feed the rail into the blade on end, keeping it flush against the fence and pushing it forward with the guide block. Repeat the cut at the other end of the rail *(left)*. Then bevel the long edges by adjusting the blade angle to 45°. Sand the rail smooth.

Making the Column

1 Turning the column. Mount a 3½-inch-square blank on your lathe and turn it with a roughing gouge followed by a spindle gouge, leaving a lip and enough stock near the bottom for the leg sockets. To help you produce the proper shape, refer to the anatomy illustration *(page 26)* and fashion yourself a template. Use a parting tool to turn the rail tenon at the top of the column, periodically checking its diameter with outside calipers *(right)*. Smooth the column with progressively finer grits of sandpaper.

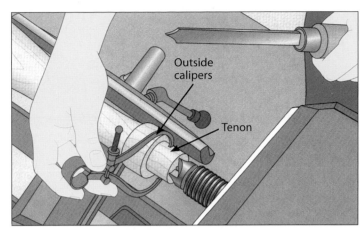

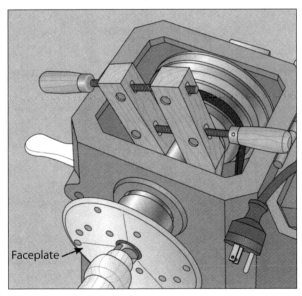

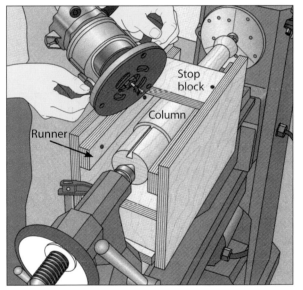

2 Routing the dovetail sockets. Unplug the lathe and cut the sockets, using a router and a shop-made jig consisting of a ¾ inch plywood box clamped to the lathe bed. Make the inside width of the box as wide as the router base plate, attaching the runners so the router bit will cut the sockets with its base plate sitting on them. Next, mark the three socket locations on the column, spacing them 120° apart. Also mark the top ends of the sockets, 3⁷⁄₁₆ inches from the bottom of the column. Transfer the socket marks to the lathe faceplate, then rotate the column by hand until one of the marks on the faceplate is vertical and immobilize the drive shaft with a handscrew *(above, left)*. Cut each socket in two steps, starting with a ¼-inch straight bit. Adjust the cutting depth to about ½ inch and, aligning the bit with the socket end mark, butt a stop block against the router base plate. Screw the block to the jig. Holding the router in both hands, feed the bit into the column at the bottom and guide the tool along the runners until the base plate contacts the stop block. Repeat with a ¼-inch dovetail bit *(above, right)*. To cut the two remaining sockets, rotate the column until the socket mark for each cut is vertical.

Making the Legs

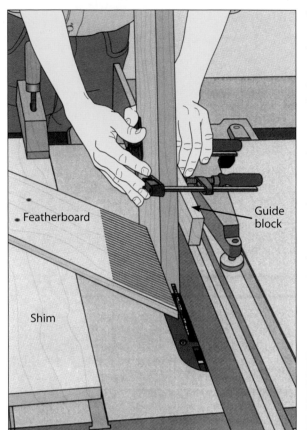

Featherboard

Guide block

Shim

1 Cutting the dovetail cheeks. Referring to the illustration below, fashion a template for the legs. The grain should follow the slope of the leg, the top and bottom ends must be perpendicular, and the spread of the legs must be less than the diameter of the top. Once the template is complete, saw along the top end of the leg on the band saw. Next, cut the dovetails in the legs in two steps, cutting the cheeks on your table saw and the shoulders by hand. Adjust the table saw's blade angle to match that of the sockets you cut in the column and set the cutting height to slightly less than the depth of the sockets. Outline the dovetails on the edge of one leg blank and, holding the blank on end on the saw table, align a cutting mark with the blade. Butt the rip fence against the stock and lock it in place. Clamp a shimmed featherboard to the table and a guide block to the blank. Make a pass to cut one cheek *(left)*, then rotate the blank and feed the opposite face along the fence to saw the other. Check the resulting dovetail against a socket in the column. If necessary, adjust the cutting width or blade angle or height and make another set of passes. Repeat for the remaining dovetails.

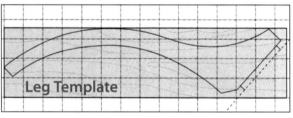

Leg Template

2 Cutting the angled shoulders. The shoulders of the leg dovetails must be cut at an angle so they lie snugly against the column (see the illustration on page 26). Once the dovetail cheeks are all cut, clamp a blank to a work surface with the cheeks extending off the table. Then use a backsaw to cut the shoulders at a slightly sharper angle than the curvature of the column *(right)*. Test-fit the dovetail in its socket and trim the socket, if necessary, until you get a suitable fit. Repeat for the remaining dovetails.

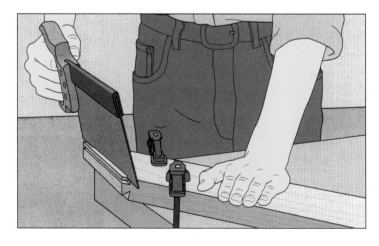

3 Shaping the legs. Cut out the legs of the candle stand on your band saw, then smooth their surfaces using a sanding block or a spindle sander *(right)*.

4 Trimming the dovetails. Trim off the top ¾ inch of each dovetail on the legs. This will hide the tops of the dovetails from view when they are pushed all the way into their sockets. Clamp the leg upright in your bench vise and mark a line on the dovetail ¾ inch from the top end. Then hold a ¼-inch chisel vertically to score the dovetail on your marked line, cutting to the shoulder. Next, holding the chisel bevel up and parallel to the dovetail shoulders, push the blade along the surface to pare away the wood in thin shavings *(left)*. Periodically test-fit the leg against the column until the shoulders rest flush against the surface.

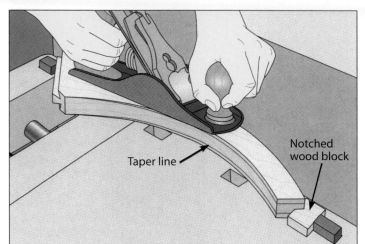

5 Tapering the legs. To give the legs an elegant appearance without sacrificing strength, taper them with a bench plane from a thickness of 1 inch at the top to ⅝ inch at the bottom. Mark taper lines along the inside edges of each leg as a planing guide. Then secure the leg face up on your bench, using a notched wood block to fix the bottom end in place. To avoid damaging your plane blade, make sure the bench dogs and the wood block are below the level of the top taper line. Starting near the top of the leg, feed the plane along the surface, increasing the downward pressure as you approach the bottom *(left)*. Continue until you cut to the taper line, then turn the leg over on the bench and repeat the process.

Taper line

Notched wood block

Assembling the Table

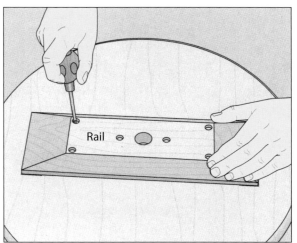

Rail

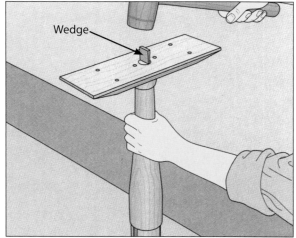

Wedge

1 Attaching the rail to the column. Start by drilling six countersunk screw holes through the rail; it will be less cumbersome to prepare the rail for the top before joining the rail and column. Locate one hole in each corner of the flat face of the rail's underside and one on each side of the mortise. Then set the top face down on a work surface and center the rail on top, making sure the grain of the two pieces is perpendicular. Mark the corners of the rail on the top with a pencil and the screw holes with an awl *(above, left)*. To prepare the column for the rail, use a backsaw to slice a kerf for a wedge in the center of the tenon to

a depth of about three-quarters the length of the tenon. Cut the kerf at a right angle to one of the dovetail sockets so the rail will be parallel to one of the legs. Cut the wedge from hardwood about 1 inch long and ⅛ inch thick at the base, tapering it to a point. To fasten the rail to the column, spread glue on their contacting surfaces and fit the pieces together with the kerf in the column tenon perpendicular to the grain of the rail. Then, holding the column upright on a work surface, apply glue in the kerf and on the wedge and hammer it in place with a wooden mallet *(above, right)*. Trim the wedge flush with the end of the tenon.

2 Fastening the legs to the column. Spread glue evenly on the dovetails and in the sockets. Then, setting the rail flat on a work surface, slide the legs into place and tap them into final position with a wooden mallet *(right)*.

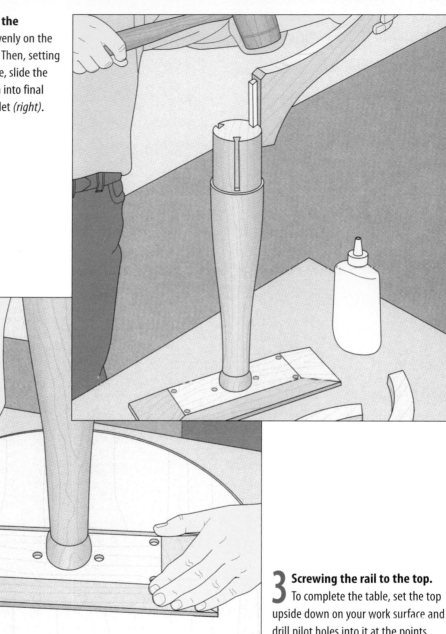

3 Screwing the rail to the top. To complete the table, set the top upside down on your work surface and drill pilot holes into it at the points you marked in step 1. Position the rail assembly on the top, aligning its corners with the marks on the surface and its screw holes with those in the top. Screw the rail in place *(left)*.

CHAPTER 4:
BLANKET CHEST

The chest is one of the earliest types of furniture, with a long utilitarian tradition. During the Middle Ages, chests served as the primary receptacles of household goods and valuables. They were also called upon to perform double duty as a seating place, at a time when chairs were a luxury for most people.

Although early chest designs were primitive, medieval artisans often adorned them with carved arches and elaborate chivalric and battle scenes. During the Renaissance and Baroque periods, the piece began to assume some of the elements that are still used today, including frame-and-panel joinery, molded tops and bases, and patterned bracket feet. Over the years, attractive hardware was added, such as brass locks, handles, and escutcheons.

In Colonial America, the chest was usually placed at the foot of a bed to store blankets, quilts, and linens—hence the name blanket chest.

Blanket chests are all relatively similar, beginning with a rectangular carcase and a hinged top. Dimensions vary, but as a general guideline consider a length of 40 to 45 inches, a width of 18 to 20 inches, and a height of about 25 inches. The carcase is made from panels of edge-glued boards and assembled with dovetail or frame-and-panel joinery. The top features routed wood strips that are attached with sliding dovetail joints or a molding can be cut into its edge. To prevent the top from warping, and as a decorative touch, wood battens can be fastened for stiffening. The top can be attached with a piano hinge or butt hinges.

You might also choose instead to install ogee bracket feet. These items should be chosen carefully to complement the particular design of your project.

A biscuit joiner cuts a slot in the mitered end of the blanket chest's molded base. The base is rabbeted to accept the carcase of the chest and the bracket feet are then screwed to the base.

This traditional dovetailed chest, with its patterned feet and molded top and bottom, is based on a design imported to America from eastern Europe in the 18th Century.

Anatomy of a Blanket Chest

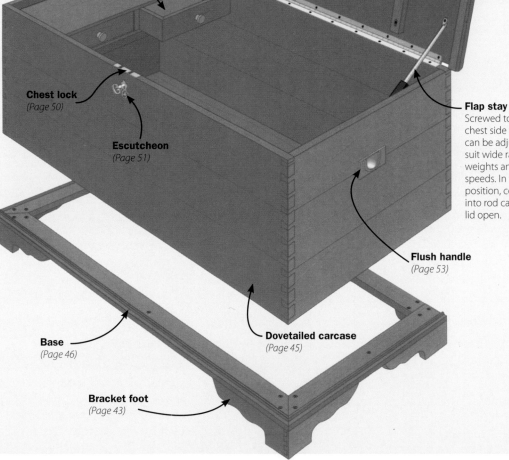
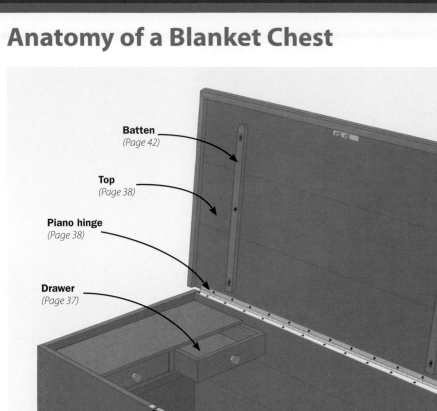

Batten
(Page 42)

Top
(Page 38)

Piano hinge
(Page 38)

Drawer
(Page 37)

Chest lock
(Page 50)

Escutcheon
(Page 51)

Flap stay
Screwed to inside of chest side and lid; can be adjusted to suit wide range of lid weights and closing speeds. In fully open position, collar snaps into rod cap to hold lid open.

Flush handle
(Page 53)

Base
(Page 46)

Dovetailed carcase
(Page 45)

Bracket foot
(Page 43)

Traditional blanket chests were often furnished with one or more drawers to store anything from papers and pens to sewing needles and thread. The top and bottom panels of the drawer assembly are mounted in stopped grooves in the front and back panels of the chest, with a divider to separate the opening for the drawers.

Inventory of Blanket Chest Hardware

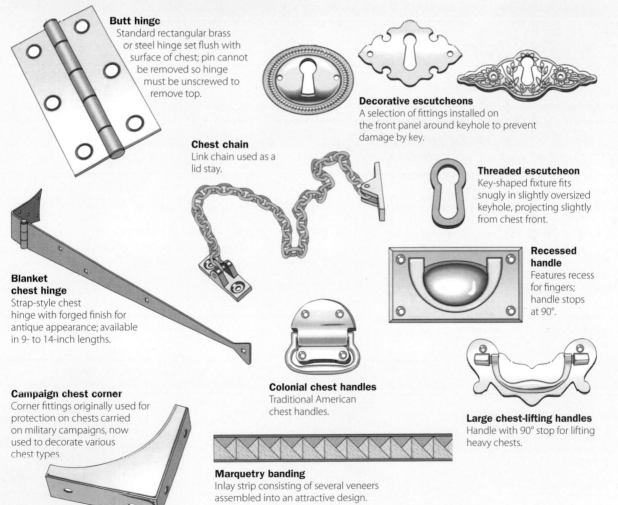

Butt hinge
Standard rectangular brass or steel hinge set flush with surface of chest; pin cannot be removed so hinge must be unscrewed to remove top.

Decorative escutcheons
A selection of fittings installed on the front panel around keyhole to prevent damage by key.

Chest chain
Link chain used as a lid stay.

Threaded escutcheon
Key-shaped fixture fits snugly in slightly oversized keyhole, projecting slightly from chest front.

Recessed handle
Features recess for fingers; handle stops at 90°.

Blanket chest hinge
Strap-style chest hinge with forged finish for antique appearance; available in 9- to 14-inch lengths.

Colonial chest handles
Traditional American chest handles.

Large chest-lifting handles
Handle with 90° stop for lifting heavy chests.

Campaign chest corner
Corner fittings originally used for protection on chests carried on military campaigns, now used to decorate various chest types.

Marquetry banding
Inlay strip consisting of several veneers assembled into an attractive design.

Tops

Since molding strips are fastened around its edges with sliding dovetails to accommodate wood movement, the chest top shown at left does not require battens to keep it flat, though two have been added for decorative effect. The lid stay holds the top open and allows it to close slowly to avoid damaging the piece.

Attaching the Top with a Piano Hinge

Installing the hinge. The hinge should be equal to or slightly shorter than the length of the chest. Clamp the top to a work surface using wood pads to protect the stock. Hold the hinge in position, aligning the center of the pin with the back edge of the top, and trace its outline. Next, install a straight bit in a router and set the cutting depth to the thickness of the hinge leaf. (Take care adjusting the depth; if the rabbet is too deep it will cause the hinge to bind when the lid is closed.) Align the bit over the inside edge of the outline, then fasten an edge guide butted against the router base plate. Rout the inside edge of the rabbet, keeping the base plate pressed against the edge guide. Make repeat cuts, adjusting the edge guide each time, until the rabbet is completed. Then, set the hinge in the rabbet and mark the location of the screw holes. If you are adding molding *(page 41)* or battens *(page 42)*, do so now. Then bore pilot holes at the marks, put the hinge back in position *(right)*, and drive the screws. Set the top on the chest, with the free hinge leaf flat on the top edge of the blanket chest's back panel. Mark the location for the screws, bore pilot holes, and drive in the screws.

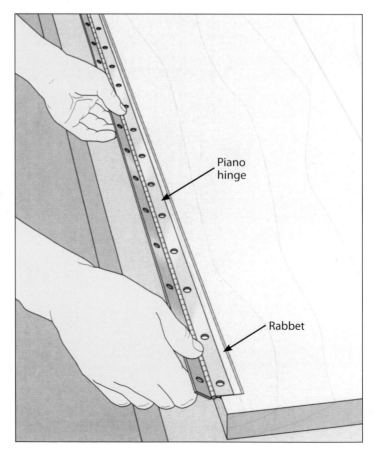

Piano hinge

Rabbet

Attaching the Top with Butt Hinges

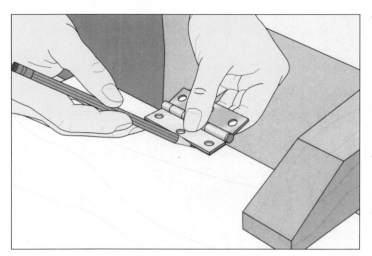

1 Tracing the hinge outlines. Instead of a piano hinge, you can use two or three butt hinges to attach the top to the blanket chest. The hinges are mortised into both the top and back panel of the chest. To begin, clamp the top good-side down on a work surface and place the first hinge in position a few inches in from one end, positioning the pin just off the back edge of the top. Use a pencil to trace the outline of the hinge *(left)*. Mark the other hinges on the top in the same manner, positioning one near the other end and one in the center, if necessary.

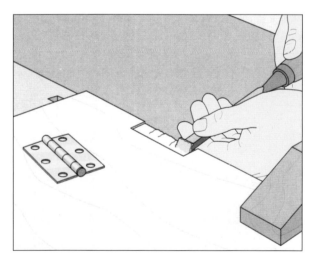

2 Chiseling out the waste. Use a chisel to score the hinge outline and cut it to the thickness of the hinge. Then, holding the chisel bevel up, pare the waste from the mortise *(above)*. Repeat the procedure to clear out the remaining mortises. Be careful to cut the mortises no deeper than the thickness of the hinge leaves to prevent binding.

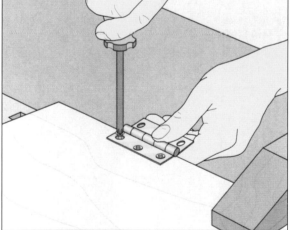

3 Installing the hinges. Set the hinges in their mortises in the top, drill pilot holes, and screw them in place *(above)*. Next, set the top on the chest, mark the location for the corresponding hinge mortises on the top edge of the back panel, then chisel them out following the procedure described in step 2. Now lay the chest on its back on a work surface and set the top good-face down behind it. Place a wood spacer slightly thicker than the top under the back of the blanket chest to line-up the free hinge leaves with their mortises. Bore pilot holes and screw the hinges in place.

Hinge Mortising Jig

A router is an ideal tool to cut mortises for your blanket chest's butt hinges, but do not try to do the job freehand. A jig like the one shown at right will guarantee fast, accurate results. You will need to equip your router with a straight bit and a template guide to make the cuts.

Make the template from a piece of ¾-inch plywood wide enough to support the router. Outline the hinge leaf on the template, being sure to compensate for the template guide and the thickness of the fence, which is also made from ¾-inch plywood. Cut out the template, then attach the fence with countersunk screws.

To use the jig, secure the top of the chest edge-up in a vise. Mark the hinge outline on the workpiece and clamp the template in position, aligning the cutout with the outline on the edge and butting the fence against

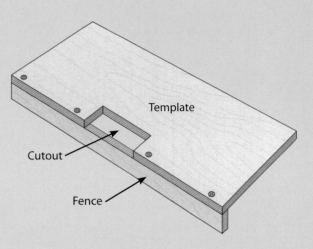

Template

Cutout

Fence

the inner face of the top. Make the cut *(below)*, moving the router in small clockwise circles until the bottom of the recess is smooth, then square the corners with a chisel. When you are using the jig to cut mortises in the top edge of the blanket chest, be sure to secure the carcase to prevent it from moving.

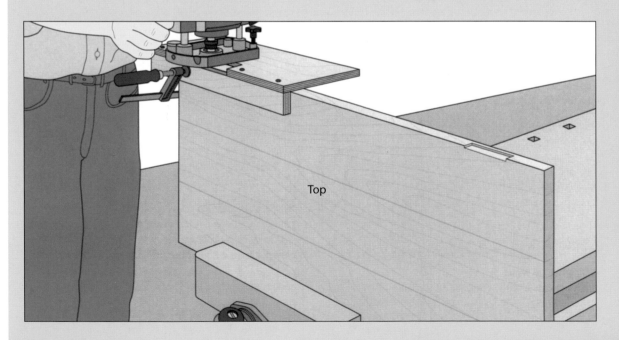

Top

Adding Molding to the Top

1 Making the molding. Install a molding bit in a router and mount the tool in a table. Rout the molding from stock thicker than the top so that when the lid is shut the molding will overhang the side and front panels slightly. (The stock should also be wider and longer than you need so that you can rip and crosscut the molding to size later.) Align the fence with the bearing and feed the board into the bit to carve the design in one half of an edge. Mount a featherboard on either side of the bit to secure the piece during the cut. (In the illustration, the front featherboard has been removed for clarity.) Flip the piece over and rout the other half, creating a mirror cut of the first *(right)*. Then rip and crosscut the molding to the size you need.

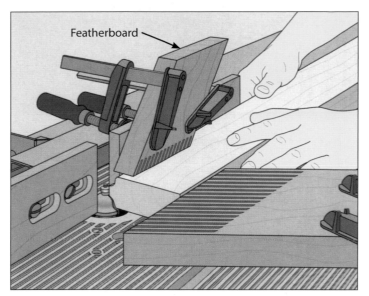

Featherboard

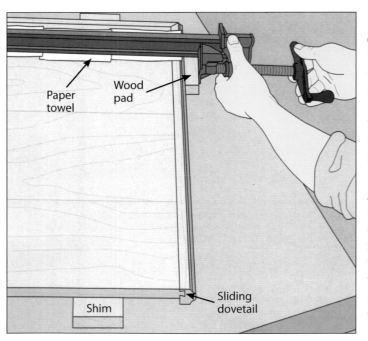

Paper towel

Wood pad

Shim

Sliding dovetail

2 Installing the molding. You can secure the molding to the edge with sliding dovetails or glue alone. In this case, the side moldings are attached with stopped sliding dovetails to allow for cross-grain wood movement; the front molding, which will shrink and swell parallel to the top panel, is attached with glue. Make stopped dovetails on the ends of the top; cut stopped dovetail mortises in the side moldings *(see page 45)*. After you have made the dovetail joints, miter the ends of the molding at 45°. Then place the top good-face up on wood shims. Spread a thin layer of glue on the last two inches of the sliding dovetail and the dovetail slot, then slide the molding into position. Next, lay some paper towel on the top to prevent scratches and install bar clamps with protective wood pads to secure the molding in place *(left)*.

Routing Molding in the Top

Top

1 Routing the edge. Instead of attaching separate strips of molding, you can rout a decorative shape in the top itself. Secure the top good-face up on a work surface with its edge projecting off the surface. Install a piloted rounding-over bit or another molding bit in your router, then set the cutting height to mold the top part of the edge. Turn on the tool and guide the bit into the stock, moving the tool against the direction of bit rotation and keeping the pilot bearing butted against the stock *(left)*. Once the top half of the edge is molded, flip the workpiece over and rout the bottom half if called for by your design.

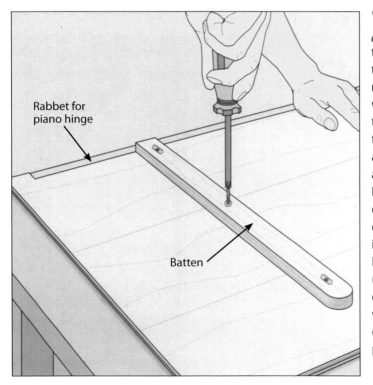

Rabbet for piano hinge

Batten

2 Adding battens. When molding is attached with sliding dovetails, it serves to stiffen the top, eliminating the need for battens; molding that is simply routed in the edge of the top does not offer this advantage. In this case, to prevent warping from changing humidity levels, fasten two or three battens across the underside of the top. Cut the strips of wood from the same stock as the top, making them about 1½ inches wide and 3 inches shorter than the width of the top. For visual appeal, round one end of each batten on the band saw. Next, set the top good-face down on a work surface and hold the first batten in place about 5 inches from one end of the top. Drive three screws to fasten it in place *(left)*. (To allow the batten to expand and contract, enlarge the counterbored holes at the ends of the wood strips into ovals; the center screw is the only one that should be driven in tight.) Repeat the process to mount the other battens.

The bottom assembly of the blanket chest consists of bracket feet mounted with screws to a rabbeted base molding that supports the carcase. The bracket feet are joined with half-blind dovetails.

Making Bracket Feet

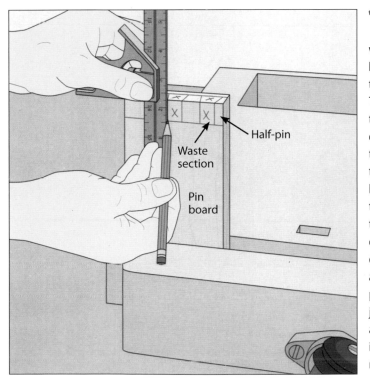

Half-pin

Waste section

Pin board

1 Marking the pin board. The feet of the blanket chest are made from two identical boards cut with a decorative scroll pattern and joined with half-blind dovetail joints. Make the joinery cuts first, then saw out the patterns and assemble the pieces. To begin, cut blanks to the size of the feet, then mark the half-blind dovetails. Indicate the outside face of each board with an X. Then adjust a cutting gauge to the thickness of the stock and scribe a line across the inside face of the pin board to mark the shoulder line. Next, secure the board end-up in a vise, set the cutting gauge to about one-third the stock's thickness, and mark a line across the end closer to its outside face. Use a dovetail square to mark the pins on the end of the board. For the size of board shown, a half-pin at each edge and two evenly spaced pins in between will make a strong and attractive joint. Indicate the waste sections with Xs, then use a combination square to extend the lines down the inside face to the shoulder line *(left)*. Repeat the marks on all the pin boards.

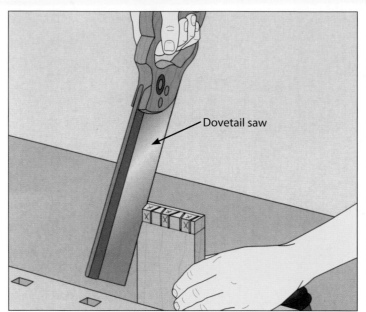

Dovetail saw

2 Cutting the pins. Secure a pin board in a vise with its outside face toward you, then cut down along the edges of the pins with a dovetail saw, working from one edge of the board to the other. For each cut, align the saw blade just to the waste side of the cutting lines *(left)*. Use smooth, even strokes, continuing the cuts to the shoulder line. Next, clamp the board outside-face down on a work surface and use a chisel and mallet to pare away the waste wood: Score a line about ⅛ inch deep along the shoulder line and then shave off a thin layer of waste, with the chisel held horizontally and bevel-up. Repeat the procedure to cut the remaining pin boards.

3 Cutting the tails. Set a cutting gauge to the thickness of the pins, then mark the shoulder line on all the tail boards. Place the first tail board outside-face down on the work surface. Hold a pin board end-down with its inside face aligned with the shoulder line of the tail board, making certain the edges of the boards are flush. Outline the tails with a pencil, then use a try square to extend the lines onto the end of the board. Mark all the waste sections with Xs. Then use a dovetail saw to cut the tails *(right)*. Angling the board, rather than the saw, makes for easier cutting. Then secure the board edge-up in the vise and cut the waste beside the two outside tails. Remove the waste between the tails with a chisel using the same technique described in step 2. When you have chiseled out half the waste, flip the piece and finish the job from the other side. Repeat the process to cut the other tail boards.

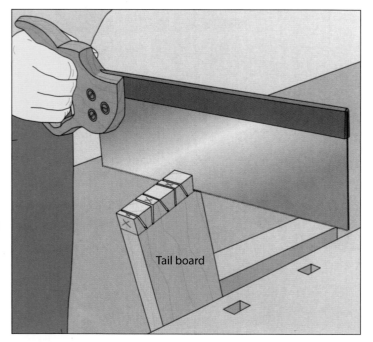

Tail board

4 **Test-fitting the joint.** Make a template with the desired pattern for the feet and trace the shape on one face of each board. Then, test-fit the half-blind dovetail joint *(right)*. Mark any spots that bind with a pencil and carefully pare some wood away at each mark until the fit is satisfactory.

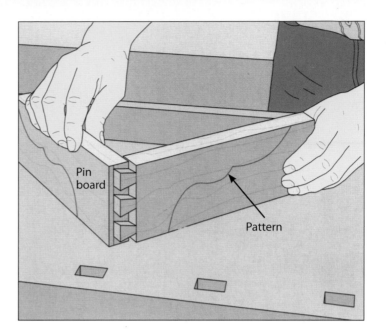

Pin board

Pattern

Cutting the Pattern

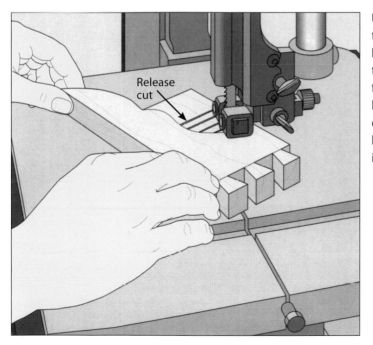

Release cut

Using the band saw. Cut the pattern in each of the feet freehand on the band saw. To keep the blade from binding in the kerf at the tight part of the curve, make a series of straight release cuts from the edge of the workpiece to the marked line. Then, align the blade just to the waste side of the cutting line and feed the workpiece into the blade with both hands, making sure neither hand is in line with the cutting edge *(left)*.

Making the Base Molding

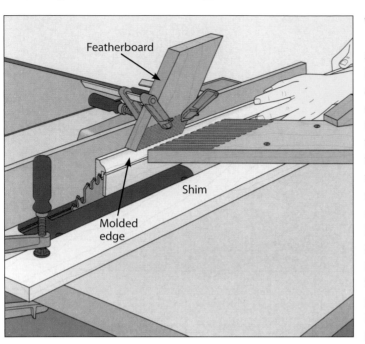

Featherboard

Shim

Molded edge

1 **Making the base pieces.** The four pieces that make up the base molding are shaped and rabbeted individually. Working with stock longer than you need, rout one edge of the front and side pieces the same way you would shape cornice molding. Next use your table saw to cut rabbets in all four pieces. The rabbets are sawn in two passes, with the shoulders first, followed by the cheeks. Adjust the blade height so the cheeks will be wide enough to support the chest without reaching the molding cuts; position the fence so one-third of the stock thickness will be cut away. Use two featherboards to support the workpiece; attach the table-mounted featherboard to a shim so the middle of the workpiece is pressed against the fence. Feed each piece on edge into the blade *(left)* until the trailing end reaches the table. Then move to the other side of the table and pull the stock past the blade.

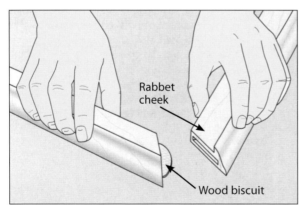

Rabbet cheek

Wood biscuit

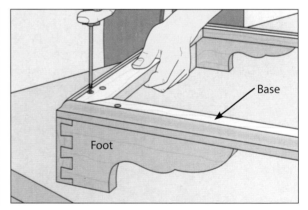

Base

Foot

2 **Gluing up the base.** Saw the molding pieces to length, cutting miters at both ends of the front piece and at one end of the sides. The front corners of the base are assembled with miter joints; butt joints are sufficient for the back. The connections should be reinforced with wood biscuits. Use a plate joiner to cut slots, then spread glue in the slots, insert biscuits in the front and back pieces, and press the corners together *(above)* and clamp them.

3 **Fastening the feet to the base.** Working on a flat surface, position the base on the feet of the chest, making sure all the outer edges are flush. At each corner, bore four countersunk holes through the base and into the foot and screw the two together *(above)*. Place the chest in the rabbets of the base piece and drive screws from underneath through the base and into the chest.

A Variation: Ogee Bracket Feet

It is easier to sand the contoured surfaces of the ogee bracket feet before installing them on the base.

Making Ogee Bracket Feet

1 Cutting the ogee cove. Ogee bracket feet are created much like the bracket feet shown on page 43, but with an S-shaped ogee profile shaped in their outside faces. Because of their contoured surfaces, the two halves of each foot are joined with a miter-and-spline joint *(page 48)*, rather than a half-blind dovetail. The ogee profile is cut in three steps on the table saw and the router. Begin by marking the profile on the end of a piece of stock long enough to make all the feet. Set up your table saw to make a cove cut in the face of the board. Use a push block to feed the stock, making several shallow passes to cut a cove of the appropriate depth *(right)*. Once you have made the cove cut, use a router fitted with a rounding-over bit to shape the corner of the board to the marked line.

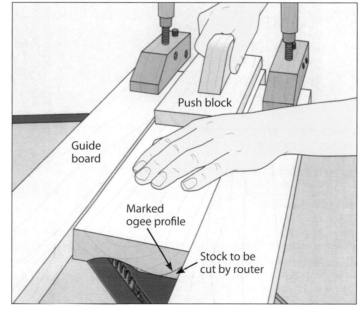

Push block

Guide board

Marked ogee profile

Stock to be cut by router

2 Finishing the ogee profile. The ridge of waste between the cove cut and the rounding-over cut is sliced off by the table saw. To set up the cut, hold the workpiece on edge on the saw table and adjust the blade angle to align the cutting edge with the marked line on the board end. Butt the rip fence against the stock, lock it in place, and set the blade height to slice away the waste. Use three featherboards to support the workpiece during the cut: Clamp two to the fence and a third to the table; this featherboard should be mounted on a shim so it will press closer to the middle of the stock against the fence. Feed the workpiece with both hands *(right)*. Once the board's trailing end reaches the table, move to the other side of the table and pull the stock past the blade.

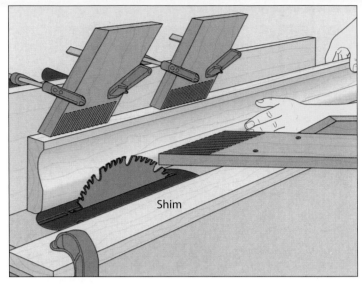

Shim

Assembling Ogee Bracket Feet

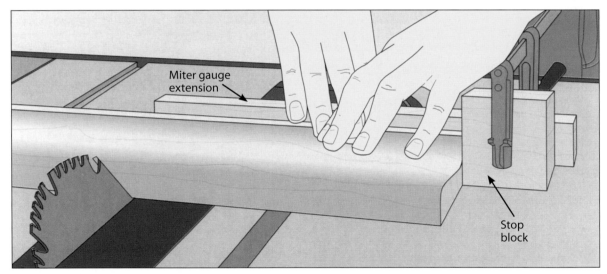

Miter gauge extension

Stop block

1 Making the bevel cuts. Since the ogee bracket feet will be assembled with miter-and-spline joints, each of the eight foot pieces will have bevels on adjoining ends. First, cut all the pieces slightly oversize. To cut the bevels, set your saw's blade angle to 45° and attach a wood extension to the miter gauge. Mark the length of a foot piece on your stock and, holding the flat edge of the board against the extension, align the mark with the blade. Before making the cut, clamp a stop block to the extension to enable you to line up the cuts for the three other identical pieces. Hold the flat edge of the board against the extension and the end against the block as you make each cut *(above)*. To bevel the ends of the four matching foot pieces, hold the contoured edge of the stock against the extension as you make the cuts.

2 **Cutting the spline grooves.**
The grooves for the splines in the beveled ends of the foot pieces are cut on the table saw. Install a dado head and adjust its thickness to that of the splines you will use. Set the angle of the head at 45° and shift the rip fence to the left-hand side of the blades. Holding one foot piece flat-face-down on the saw table, butt the beveled end against the cutting edges of the dado head and adjust the fence and blade height so a ⅜-inch groove will be located about ¼ inch from the bottom of the piece. Butt the fence against the end of the stock and lock it in place. Feed each piece with the miter gauge *(left)*, pressing the end against the fence throughout the cut.

3 **Cutting the patterns and gluing up the feet.** Once all the spline grooves are cut, design the scroll patterns on the flat faces of the pieces and cut them out on the band saw *(page 45)*. Sand the pieces smooth, then cut splines from plywood or solid wood to fit into the grooves. The splines should be as long as the grooves; make their width slightly less than twice the combined depth of two grooves. (If you use solid wood for the splines, cut them so the grain runs across their width, rather than lengthwise.) Spread adhesive in the grooves and glue up the feet *(right)*, then attach them to the base as you would standard bracket feet *(page 46)*.

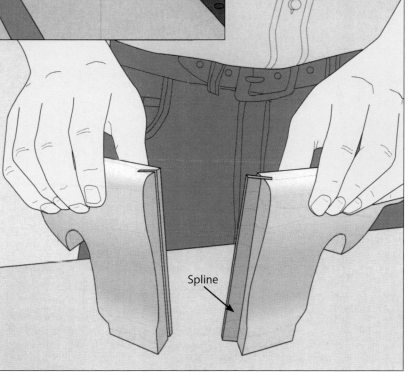

Spline

A common feature of traditional campaign chests, solid brass flush handles add a touch of class to any blanket chest. The handles stop at a 90° angle to the sides of the chest, providing a convenient way to lift the piece.

Installing a Lock

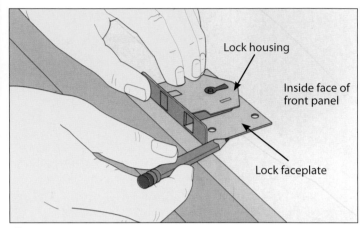

Lock housing

Inside face of front panel

Lock faceplate

1 Outlining the lock faceplate. Lay the chest on its front panel and position the lock face-down midway between the sides and flush with the top edge of the panel. Trace the outline of the faceplate *(above)*, then extend the lines onto the top edge of the panel.

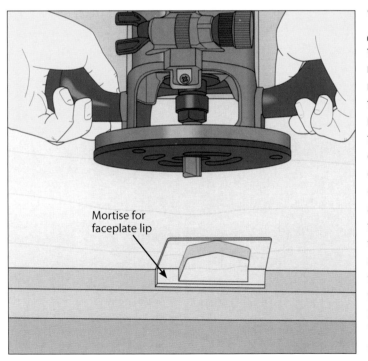

Mortise for faceplate lip

2 Routing the lock mortise. This is one of the rare instances in which the router is used to make a freehand cut. Care and patience are required. Use a wood chisel to first cut a shallow mortise for the faceplate lip in the top edge of the front panel. Next, install a straight bit in your router, set the cutting depth to the thickness of the faceplate, and cut a mortise inside the marked outline. Start by guiding the tool in a clockwise direction to cut the outside edges of the mortise; clear out the remaining waste by feeding the tool against the direction of bit rotation. Use the chisel to square the corners and pare to the line. Measure the distance between the edges of the faceplate and the lock housing and transfer the measurement to the mortise. Adjust the router's cutting depth to the thickness of the housing and cut the final mortise *(left)*. Use the chisel to square any corners. Test-fit the lock in the cavity and use the chisel to deepen or widen any of the mortises, if necessary.

3 **Cutting the keyhole.** Set the lock in the mortise and mark the location of the keyhole. Cut the opening by drilling one hole for the key shaft and another for the key bit. Use a small file to join the two holes *(right)*.

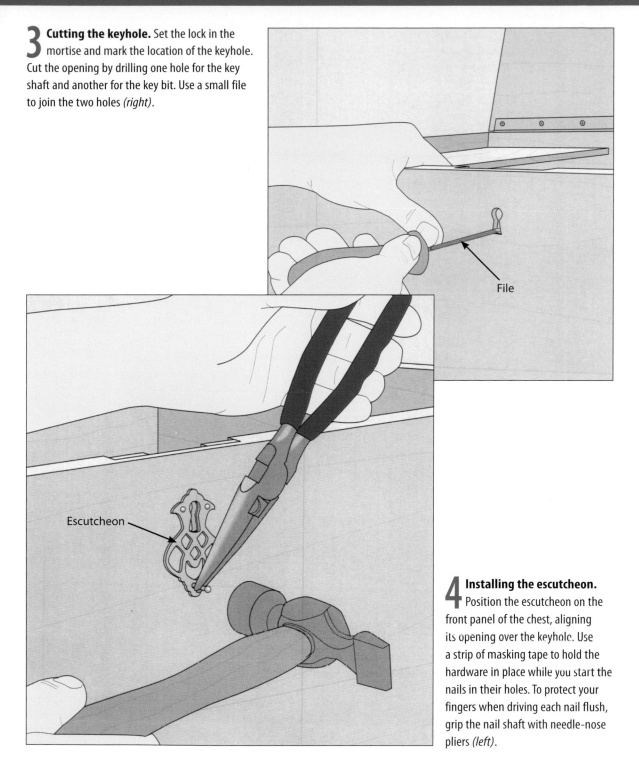

File

Escutcheon

4 **Installing the escutcheon.** Position the escutcheon on the front panel of the chest, aligning its opening over the keyhole. Use a strip of masking tape to hold the hardware in place while you start the nails in their holes. To protect your fingers when driving each nail flush, grip the nail shaft with needle-nose pliers *(left)*.

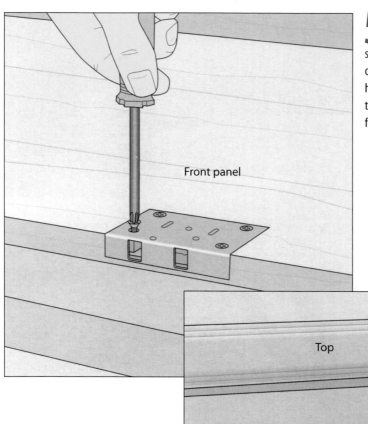

Front panel

5 **Mounting the lock.** Once the keyhole is cut, lay the chest on its front panel again and set the lock in its mortise. Mark the screw holes on the panel, remove the lock, and bore pilot holes. Set the lock in place again and fasten it to the chest, driving the screw heads flush with the faceplate *(left)*.

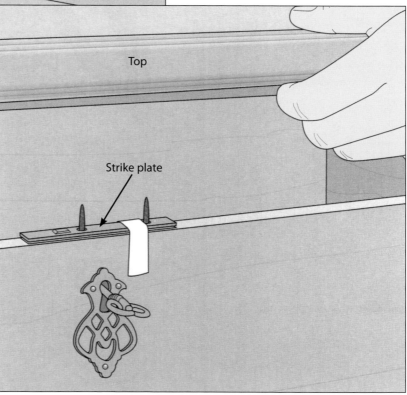

Top

Strike plate

6 **Installing the strike plate.** Complete the lock installation by mounting the strike plate to the top of the chest. Slip the screws through their holes in the plate and set the plate on top of the lock. Turn the key until the lock engages with the strike plate, then add a strip of masking tape to hold the plate firmly in place. Slowly close the top of the chest *(right)* until its underside touches the screws. Bore a pilot hole at each mark left by the screw tips and attach the strike plate to the top.

Installing Flush Handles

1 Outlining the handles. Lay the chest on one side and position a handle outside-face-down midway between the front and back panels and a few inches below the top. Trace the outline of the mounting plate *(right)*.

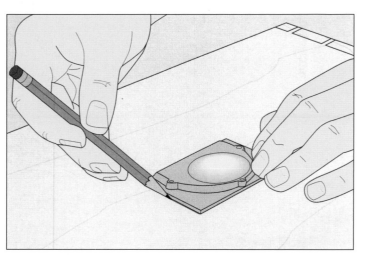

2 Mounting the handles. Install a straight bit in your router, set the cutting depth to the thickness of the mounting plate, and cut a mortise inside the marked outline as you would for a lock *(page 50)*. Next, measure the distance between the edges of the mounting plate and the bowl-shaped housing and transfer the measurement to the mortise. Adjust the router's cutting depth to the thickness of the housing and cut the deeper mortise. Test-fit the handle in the cavity and use a wood chisel to pare any remaining waste wood from the mortises *(far left)*. Once the mounting plate rests flush with the outside face of the side panel, mark the screw holes, remove the handle, and bore a pilot hole at each mark. Set the handle in place again and fasten it to the chest *(near left)*. Repeat the procedure for the other handle.

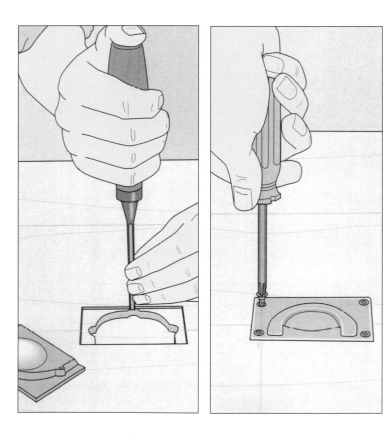

Inlays

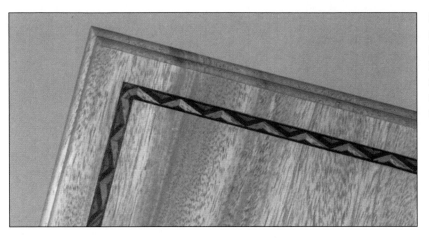

Commercial banding is available in a variety of designs to complement works ranging from a Welsh dresser to a boardroom table. Here, it adds a decorative touch to the top of a blanket chest. Inlay materials can be metal, wood veneer, or solid hardwood.

Installing Inlay

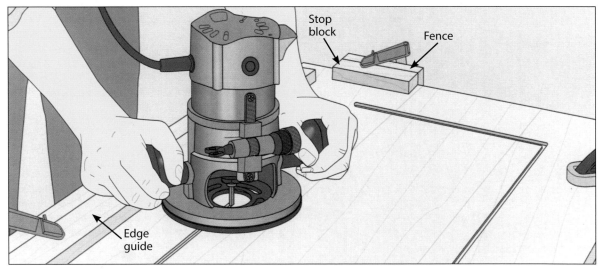

Stop block

Fence

Edge guide

1 **Routing the groove.** Grooves for inlay are cut with a router fitted with a straight bit the same width as the inlay. If you are installing shop-made inlay, set the cutting depth slightly shallower than the thickness of the strips; the inlay will be sanded flush *(step 3)*. For commercial banding, which is very thin, make the cutting depth equal to the inlay thickness to minimize sanding. Outline the groove on the top with a pencil; it should be equidistant from the edges. Rout the four sides of the groove individually, guiding the tool with an L-shaped edge guide and stop blocks. To set up the guides, align the bit with

the cutting line, measure the distance between the router base plate and the edge of the top, and cut the edge guide and stop blocks to that width. Screw a fence to each piece so it can be positioned square to the edges of the top. For each cut, clamp the guide along the edge you will be cutting and fasten a stop block at each end. Holding the router's base plate against the edge guide and one stop block, turn on the tool and plunge the bit into the stock. Feed the bit *(above)* until the base plate contacts the other stop block. Once all the cuts are made, square the corners with a chisel.

2 Setting the inlay in the groove. Cut the inlay to length to fit in the groove, using your table saw for shop-made inlay, or a wood chisel for commercial banding. For the rectangular groove shown, make 45° miter cuts at the ends of the inlay pieces. Cut and test-fit one piece at a time, then spread a little glue on the underside of the inlay and insert it in the slot *(right)*, tapping the strip gently with a wooden mallet. Commercial banding should be held in place with masking tape until the adhesive cures.

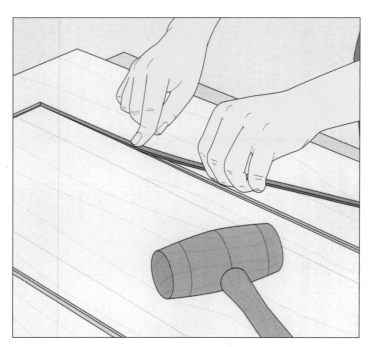

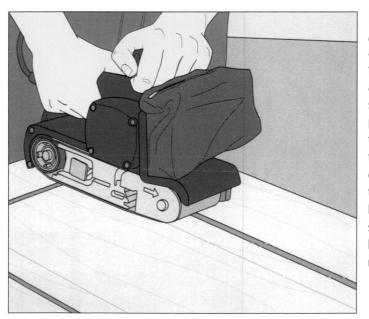

3 Trimming the inlay. Once the glue has dried, sand the top to remove any excess adhesive and bring the inlay perfectly flush with the surface of the wood. For shop-made inlay, use a belt sander fitted with a 120-grit belt. Move the sander forward along one inlay piece *(left)* and pull the sander back when you reach the end of the strip, overlapping the first pass by one-half the width of the belt. Continue until the surfaces of the inlay and the top are flush, then move on to the other strips. Repeat the process with a finer belt (150- or 180-grit) to smooth the inlay and the surrounding surface. Sand commercial banding by hand with a sanding block. Be careful: Some modern banding is less than $\frac{1}{20}$ inch thick.

CHAPTER 5:
FOUR-POSTER BED

The four-poster bed is a dramatic and imposing piece of furniture that descends from the canopy beds of the Byzantine and medieval periods. Once, only heads of families could occupy a bed with a full canopy; others contented themselves with half-canopy beds, or unadorned beds.

The use of a canopied bed conveyed some practical benefits as well. The heavily quilted drapery that hung from the framework of boards called testers provided privacy. The folds of fabric also shut out the cold winter drafts that were common and, in summer, the drapes were replaced by light netting to keep insects at bay. In its undraped form, the four-poster style has been an American favorite for almost 200 years.

The only real change in four-poster design occurred relatively recently, with the advent of box springs and spring mattresses. Before, a mattress was placed directly on a platform of rope stretched tightly between the bed rails. To resist the tension of the cords, the rails had to be quite stout—as much as 3 inches thick. Box springs, however, could be laid on narrow cleats fastened to the inside of the rails, so the rails themselves could be reduced to a mere 1 inch thick.

The most prominent feature of the bed are its four posts, each standing well over 6 feet tall. Given the 36-inch capacity of the typical lathe, turning the posts can seem to be an intimidating prospect. But, as shown on page 60, you can divide each post into four manageable segments and turn them separately. By introducing decorative elements like beads and coves adjacent to the joint lines, the breaks are not noticeable and the posts appear to be solid turnings.

Two sections of a bed post are being fitted together with a long mortise-and-tenon known as a tang joint. Located to coincide with decorative elements on the posts, the joints are virtually invisible. This one is not glued together, but assembled dry so the bed can be easily disassembled and transported.

Whether they are graced by a canopy of hanging drapery or left bare, the uprights and testers of a four-poster bed are impressive. The mahogany bed shown at left also features a sunrise headboard.

Anatomy of a Four-Poster Bed

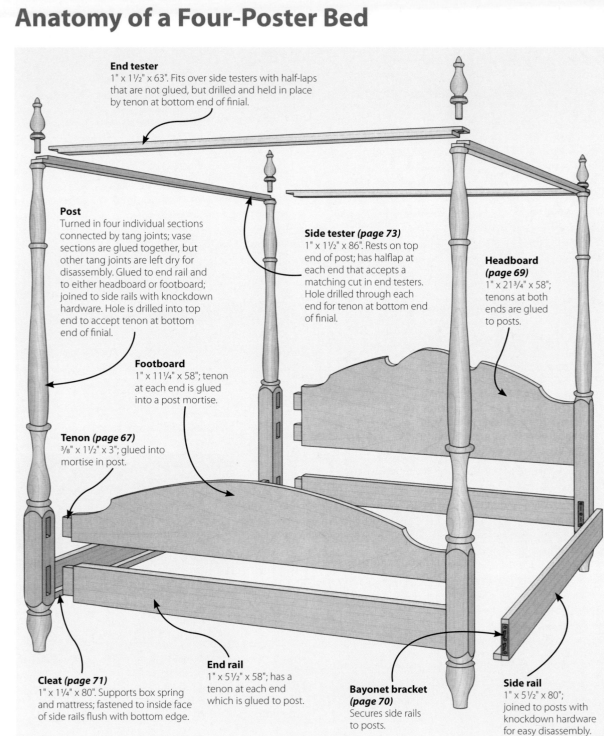

End tester
1" x 1½" x 63". Fits over side testers with half-laps that are not glued, but drilled and held in place by tenon at bottom end of finial.

Post
Turned in four individual sections connected by tang joints; vase sections are glued together, but other tang joints are left dry for disassembly. Glued to end rail and to either headboard or footboard; joined to side rails with knockdown hardware. Hole is drilled into top end to accept tenon at bottom end of finial.

Side tester *(page 73)*
1" x 1½" x 86". Rests on top end of post; has halflap at each end that accepts a matching cut in end testers. Hole drilled through each end for tenon at bottom end of finial.

Headboard
(page 69)
1" x 21¾" x 58"; tenons at both ends are glued to posts.

Footboard
1" x 11¼" x 58"; tenon at each end is glued into a post mortise.

Tenon *(page 67)*
⅜" x 1½" x 3"; glued into mortise in post.

Cleat *(page 71)*
1" x 1¼" x 80". Supports box spring and mattress; fastened to inside face of side rails flush with bottom edge.

End rail
1" x 5½" x 58"; has a tenon at each end which is glued to post.

Bayonet bracket
(page 70)
Secures side rails to posts.

Side rail
1" x 5½" x 80"; joined to posts with knockdown hardware for easy disassembly.

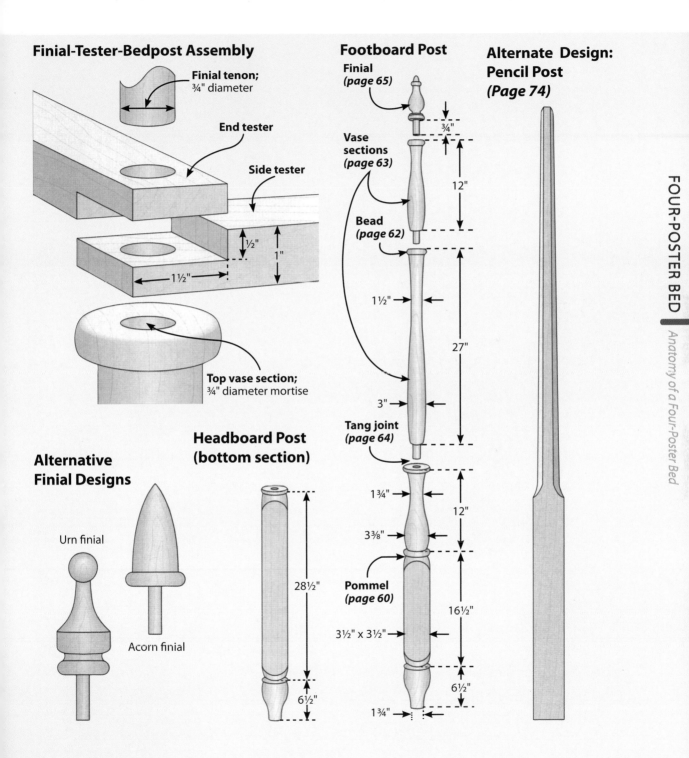

Finial-Tester-Bedpost Assembly

Finial tenon;
¾" diameter

End tester

Side tester

½"

1"

1½"

Top vase section;
¾" diameter mortise

Alternative
Finial Designs

Urn finial

Acorn finial

Headboard Post
(bottom section)

28½"

6½"

Footboard Post

Finial
(page 65)

¾"

Vase
sections
(page 63)

12"

Bead
(page 62)

1½"

27"

3"

Tang joint
(page 64)

1¾"

12"

3⅜"

Pommel
(page 60)

3½" x 3½"

16½"

6½"

1¾"

Alternate Design:
Pencil Post
(Page 74)

FOUR-POSTER BED *Anatomy of a Four-Poster Bed*

Turning the Bedposts

Turning the bedposts of a four-poster bed may appear to be a daunting challenge, but the project is manageable if broken down into its component parts. The design of the posts is simple; each one comprises only a few recurring elements, such as pommels, beads, vases, and tenons. See the anatomy illustrations on page 59 for details of the posts' diameters and the locations of the various elements. Each 6-foot-long post is turned in four individual sections, allowing for the 36-inch limit of most lathes. Since the sections are joined by tang joints, remember to allow for the 2-inch-long tenons when cutting your blanks to length.

Although the bottom sections of the footboard and headboard posts are different, the four posts are otherwise identical. Turn their matching sections one after another, rather than producing an entire post before moving on to the next one. Start with the bottom sections, and move up, turning the vase sections *(page 63)* next and the finials *(page 65)* last.

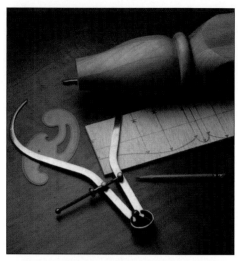

The pommel, or bottom section, of a four-poster bedpost is turned using a story pole and calipers. It includes key dimensions and diameters as well as decorative elements like beads. A French curve is a good design tool for drawing on the pole. The calipers are used to check the size of the blanks as turning proceeds.

Making the Pommel Sections

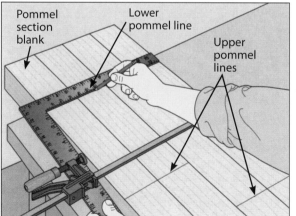

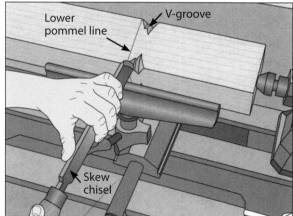

1 Defining the pommels. Cut the four pommel-section blanks to size, then outline the pommels. Set the stock on a work surface and clamp the pieces together ends aligned so you can mark all the pommels at the same time. The lower pommels are at the same height on all four pieces. Mount one of the blanks between centers on your lathe and adjust the

machine's speed to slow. Starting about ½ inch outside the lower pommel line, turn a V-groove into the corners of the blank with a skew chisel *(above, right)*. Deepen the groove until it runs completely around the workpiece. To avoid kickback, cut with the point of the blade with the bevel rubbing against the stock.

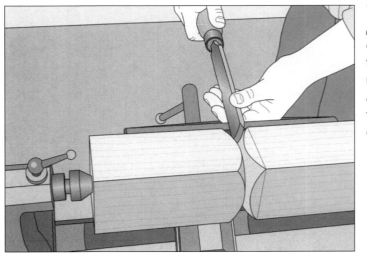

2 Shaping the pommel. Once you have finished the V-groove, widen it gradually, cutting with the long point of the chisel pointed forward. Roll the chisel from side to side while raising the handle so the bevel continues rubbing against the edges of the groove walls as you cut them *(left)*. Turn off the lathe after each cut to check the shape of the pommel.

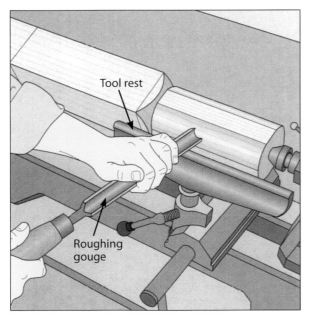

Tool rest

Roughing gouge

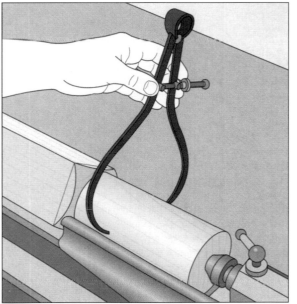

3 Turning the cylindrical part of the post. Once the pommel is finished, use a roughing-out gouge to turn the cylindrical portion of the post below the pommel. Holding the gouge with an overhand grip, brace it on the tool rest. Cut very lightly into the blank, making sure the bevel is rubbing against the stock and moving the gouge smoothly along the tool rest. As the gouge begins rounding the corners

of the post *(above, left)*, make successively deeper passes along the blank, raising the handle of the tool slightly with each pass, until the edges are completely rounded and you have a cylinder. Adjust the position of the tool rest as you progress to keep it close to the blank and periodically check the diameter of the bottom segment of the post with calipers *(above, right)*.

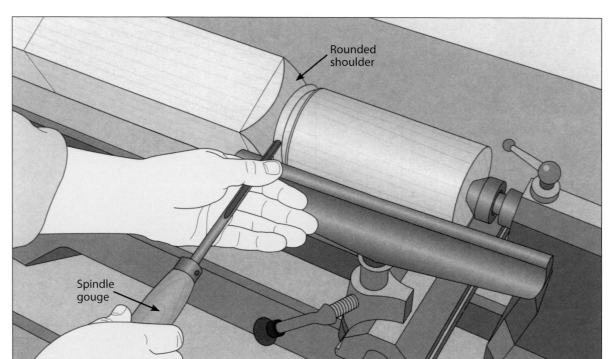

Rounded shoulder

Spindle gouge

4 **Turning the bead.** Use a pencil to outline the bead between the lower pommel and cylindrical section of the post, then make a V-cut at each line with a skew chisel. Switch to a spindle gouge to finish the bead. Beginning at the center—or highest point—of the bead, hold the gouge flat and perpendicular to the post so its bevel is rubbing. Raise the handle and make a downhill cut—working from a high point to a low point—rotating the tool in the direction of the cut and angling the handle away *(above)*. The gouge should finish the cut resting on its side. Repeat for the other side of the bead, angling and rolling the tool in the opposite direction. Round the shoulders of the bead by blending it into the turning. Once the bead is finished, continue turning the bottom segment of the post until it has the shape shown on page 59. Repeat the process to turn beads at the upper pommel line and for both pommels of the remaining posts.

Shop Tip

Using preset calipers
Since you are turning the various sections of the bedposts to different diameters, you can speed up the process by adjusting separate calipers for each feature of the blanks. For the turning shown at right, one pair is adjusted for the thicker part of the cylindrical segment, another is set for the bead below it, and a third is adjusted for the narrow section near the bottom of the workpiece. This will save you the trouble of continually readjusting a single pair of calipers. To avoid confusing the settings, attach a numbered strip of tape to each instrument.

Turning the Vase Sections

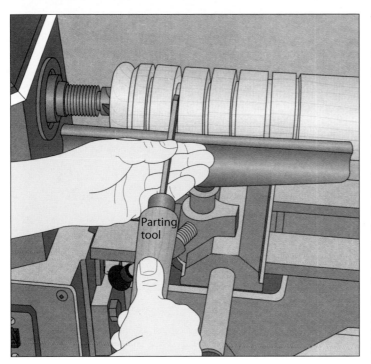

Parting
tool

1 **Making sizing cuts.** Once the lower pommel sections of the four posts are done, turn to the vase sections. Each post has three vase segments: one at the top of the pommel section and two more above it. Although the bottommost one is the widest and the next one up is longest, the vases are otherwise identical and have similar contours. They also feature a tenon at the bottom end and a matching mortise at the top. To produce a vase, turn the segment into a cylinder *(page 61)*, then make a series of sizing cuts with a parting tool. Holding the parting tool with an underhand grip edge-up on the tool rest, raise the handle slightly so the blade cuts into the cylinder. Continue to raise the handle until the cut reaches the required depth *(left)*. Each cut should penetrate to the finished diameter of the post at that point; check your progress with calipers periodically. Twist the tool slightly from side to side as you make the cut to minimize friction and to prevent the blade from jamming.

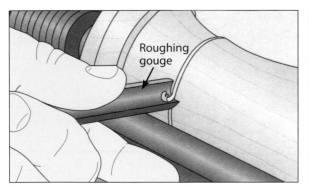

Roughing
gouge

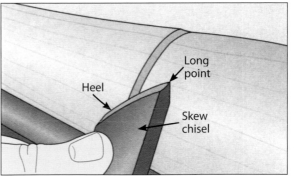

Long
point

Heel

Skew
chisel

2 **Roughing out the vase.** Once you have finished all the sizing cuts, use a roughing gouge to clear out the waste between cuts. Follow the same procedure you would use to turn a cylinder, holding the tool with an overhand grip and always working in a downhill direction to avoid tearout *(above)*. Joining the sizing cuts will create a taper along the length of the workpiece. Use a spindle gouge to round over the ends of the vase.

3 **Planing the vase smooth.** Use a skew chisel to smooth the vase. Holding the tool with an underhand grip and with the lathe turned off, set the blade on the tool rest so that its long point is above the blank and its bevel is inclined in the direction of the cut; this is about 65° to the axis of the wood. Switch on the lathe and raise the handle slightly, bringing the cutting edge of the chisel into contact with the stock. Move the blade along the tool rest *(above)*, letting its bevel rub; do not allow the heel or long point dig into the wood. The center of the cutting edge should produce a series of thin shavings.

Making the Tang Joints

1 Turning the tenons. Once you have turned all the vases, it is time to produce the tang joints. Start by turning tenons at the bottom ends of the two separate vase sections and finial blank. Mark the tenon shoulder 2 inches from the end of the workpiece by holding a pencil against the spinning blank. Then, holding a parting tool with an underhand grip, make a series of sizing cuts to define the tenon *(page 63)*. Use a roughing gouge to clear out the waste between the cuts. As the tenon begins to take shape, periodically check it with calipers, stopping when the tenon is ¾ inch in diameter. Finally, use a skew chisel to undercut the shoulder slightly; this will ensure that the bottom ends of the vase sections sit flush on the sections below without wobbling. Hold the chisel edge-up so its long point and bevel are aligned with the shoulder line. Then slowly raise and twist the handle, slicing deeper into the shoulder as the cutting edge approaches the tenon *(right)*.

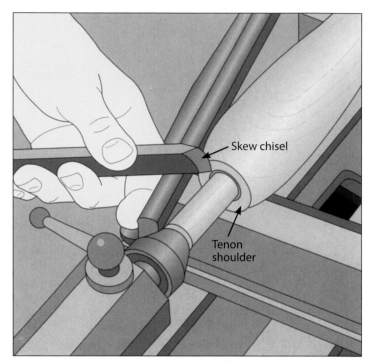

Skew chisel

Tenon shoulder

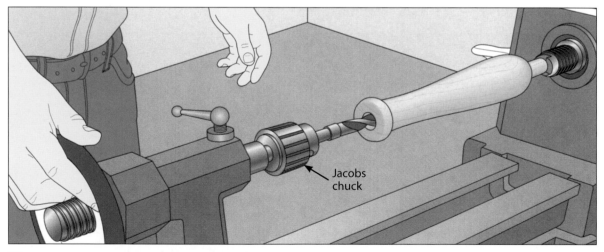

Jacobs chuck

2 Boring the mortises. Remove the blank and tool rest, and adjust the lathe to its slowest speed. Mount a ¾-inch drill bit in a Jacobs chuck and attach the chuck to the lathe tailstock. Mount the tenon-end of the blank in the headstock and slide the tailstock along the bed until the bit meets the center of the workpiece. Then turn on the lathe and turn the handwheel to advance the tailstock so the bit bores straight into the end of the blank *(above)*; be sure to hold the workpiece steady at the start of the operation.

Turning the Finials

1 Shaping the finials. The finials at the top of the bedposts combine vases and beads. After turning these elements, separate the top end of the finial from the waste wood used to hold the blank between centers. To avoid marring the finial's rounded top, use a skew chisel to part off the workpiece. Holding the tool with an underhand grip, make a slicing cut with the long point of the blade as you would round a pommel *(page 61)*. Make a series of deeper V-cuts *(right)*. Before the finished turning breaks loose from the waste, support it with one free hand, keeping your fingers well clear of the tool rest and being careful not to grip the spinning workpiece.

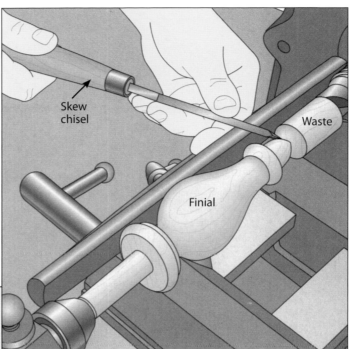

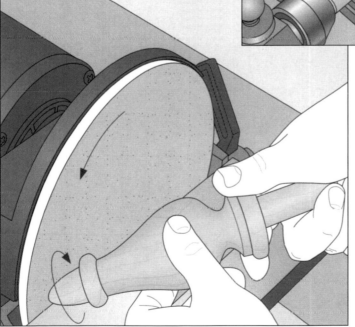

2 Smoothing the finial. To remove any tool marks left on the finials by the skew chisel, sand their surfaces smooth. You can do the job by hand, securing the stock in a bench vise and using a sanding block. But a disk sander like the one shown at left will make quick work of the task. Holding the finial on the sanding table, ease it into the disk at an angle of about 45°. Applying light pressure, rotate the finial until it is smooth.

2 Marking the edges of the tenons. Once all the tenon cheeks have been cut, mark the tenons' edges, using their post mortises as a guide. Outline single tenons on the end rails and footboard; the headboard, shown at right, has two tenons. Set the post on a work surface with its mortises facing up and position the mating piece on top, aligning the end of the board with the mortises. Then, line up the blade of a combination square with one end of a mortise and, holding the handle of the square against the end of the tenon and the tip of the blade against the shoulder, mark the tenon edge across the cheek with a pencil. Outline the remaining tenon edges the same way *(right)*, marking the waste with Xs as you go.

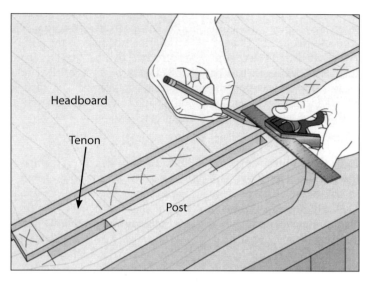

Headboard

Tenon

Post

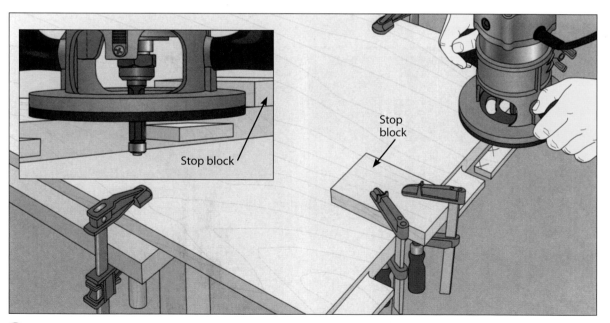

Stop block

Stop block

3 Finishing the tenons. Clear the waste adjoining the edges of the tenons using a router fitted with a bottom-piloted flush-trimming bit. Clamp the stock to a work surface and align the cutter with the edge of a tenon. Then butt a stop block against the router base plate and clamp it to the workpiece. If there is a second tenon on the same end of the stock, as in the headboard, clamp a second stop block to prevent the router from cutting into the tenon. With the tool's base plate flat on the workpiece and flush against the stop block, ease the bit into the stock until the pilot bearing reaches the tenon shoulder. Feed the router along the end of the board, stopping when the base plate contacts a second stop block *(inset)* or the bit reaches the edge of the workpiece *(above)*. Clean up the edges of the tenon with a chisel.

Shaping the End Boards

1 Making the end board templates. Shape the curved profiles of the head-and footboards with a router guided by templates. Make the templates from ¾-inch plywood, tracing the contours of the boards' top edges, as illustrated on page 58, on the plywood. But instead of producing templates that span the full end boards, mark only one-half the patterns on the templates, from one end to the middle; not only will the templates be easier to maneuver, but by using a single pattern to outline both halves of each board, you will ensure that they are symmetrical. Cut each pattern one-half as long as the end board, plus about 12 inches. On both sides of the template, mark one end of the end board, then the middle, and trace the curved pattern in between. Cut the pattern on your band saw, then smooth the cut edge, using a spindle sander *(right)* or a sanding block.

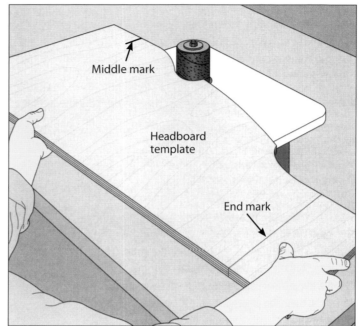

Middle mark

Headboard template

End mark

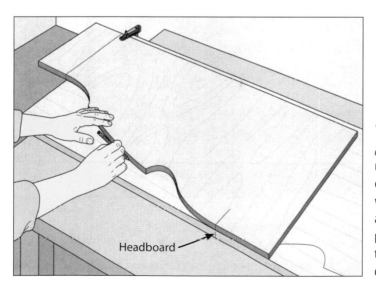

Headboard

2 Marking the end board stock. Set the stock face-up on a work surface and mark the middle on the top edge. Then clamp the template on top, aligning the end mark with the end of the workpiece and the two middle marks. Run a pencil along the cut edge of the template to outline the pattern on the end board stock *(left)*. Then turn the template over and repeat the process to mark the other half of the workpiece.

Gluing up the Bedposts and End Boards

1 Gluing the bedpost vase sections together.
Although the joints connecting the pommel sections and finials of the posts to the vase sections are not glued, the tang joints between the vase sections must be glued to give the posts adequate rigidity. For maximum flexibility at glue-up, use white glue rather than yellow adhesive; it takes longer to set, allowing more time for adjustment after it has been applied. Spread adhesive on the tenon and in the mortise of the tang joint and on the contacting surfaces between the two pieces, then secure them in a bar clamp, protecting the stock with wood pads. If the post begins to distort as you tighten the clamp, reposition it in the jaws until it remains straight. Keep tightening *(right)* until a glue bead squeezes out of the joint.

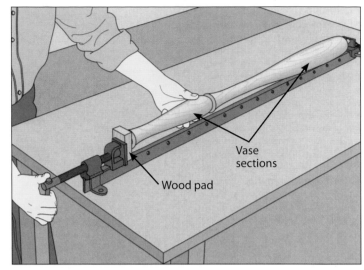

Vase sections

Wood pad

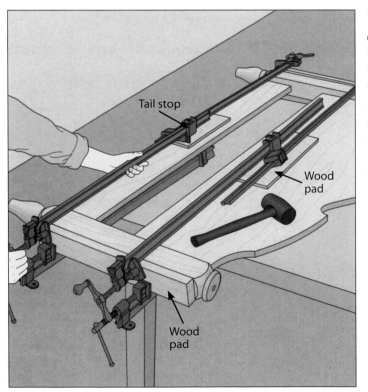

Tail stop

Wood pad

Wood pad

2 Gluing the posts to the end boards.
Set the end boards with their respective end rails and posts on a work surface, and test-fit the mortise-and-tenon joints between them. Use a chisel to pare away wood from any ill-fitting joints. Apply glue to the contacting surfaces of the posts and end boards and rails, and use a non-marring dead-blow hammer to tap the joints together, if necessary. Secure the pieces with four long pipe clamps or eight shorter bar clamps used in pairs, as shown at left. Position two clamps across the end board so the handle-end jaws rest against opposite posts and the tail stops of the clamps overlap. Protect the posts with wood pads cut as long and wide as the pommel sections; use plywood pads to protect the faces of the end boards and rails. Tighten one of the clamps until the tail stops make contact. Repeat with two more clamps across the end rail and partially tighten all four clamps, then turn the assembly over and install the remaining four clamps. Tighten all the clamps *(left)* until a thin glue bead squeezes out of the joints.

Making and Installing the Testers

1 **Notching the ends of the testers.** Once the bedposts, end boards, and rails are glued up and assembled, it is time to prepare the testers that connect the top ends of the posts. Use your table saw to cut the half-laps that join the testers. Install a dado head, adjusting it to its maximum width, and set the cutting height at one-half the stock thickness. Screw an extension board to the miter gauge. Position the rip fence for a width of cut equal to the width of the testers, then cut each half-lap in two passes. Start by aligning the end of the board with the dado head and, holding the edge of the tester flush against the miter gauge extension, feed the stock into the cut. Make the second pass the same way, but with the end of the board flush against the fence *(right)*.

Miter gauge extension

Tester

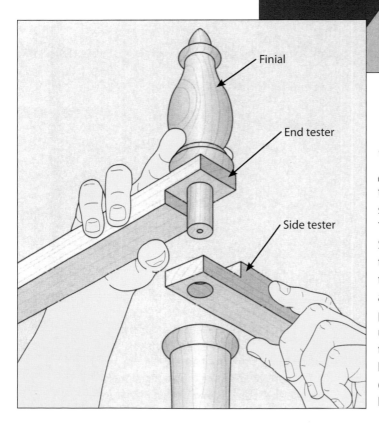

Finial

End tester

Side tester

2 **Installing the testers.** Bore a hole through the center of each half-lap at the end of the testers, using your drill press fitted with a bit the same diameter as the finial tenons—¾ inch. To prevent tearout, bore the holes in two steps: Start by drilling halfway through the stock, then turn the tester over and complete the hole from the other side. (You can also assemble the testers and drill the two holes at the same time with a portable drill. This will ensure that the holes line up perfectly.) Install the testers at one corner of the bed at a time. Slip the finial tenon through the hole in the end tester and, holding the side tester over the bedpost *(left)*, fit the tenon through its hole into the mortise in the post.

Pencil Posts

The tapered octagonal bedpost, known as a pencil post, is a popular alternative to the turned version featured in the previous section. To avoid tearout as you shape the posts, make your blanks from 3½-inch-thick stock with straight grain; if you choose to glue up thinner boards to make up the blanks, make sure the wood grain of the pieces runs in the same direction.

Shaping the octagonal sections of the posts is a challenge of design and execution. The bevels that create the octagon must be laid out so the eight sides are equal as the post tapers from base to tip. Although the layout method shown below is straightforward, it demands precise drafting.

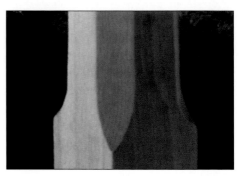

With its solid, square base giving way to an octagonal section that gradually tapers to a narrow tip, the pencil post shown above offers both strength and refinement. The curved bevels that mark the transition between the square and octagonal segments are known as lamb's tongues.

Making Pencil Posts

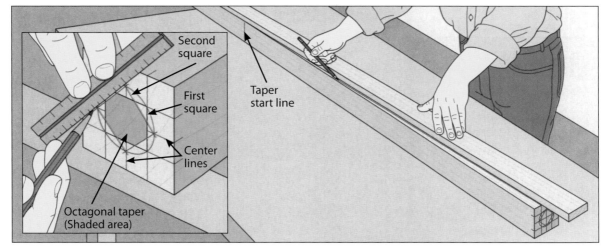

Second square

First square

Taper start line

Center lines

Octagonal taper (Shaded area)

1 Outlining the tapers. For a bed of the dimensions shown on page 58, mark a line for the start of the taper all around the blank 20 inches from the bottom end. Then start by centering a 1¼-inch square on the end with sides parallel to the stock's side. Extend the sides of the square to the edges of the stock, then draw vertical and horizontal lines through the center, each bisecting the square's sides. Next use a compass to draw a circle from the center of the square that passes through each of its four corners. Then, with a pencil and ruler, draw a second square whose corners meet where the circle and center lines intersect *(inset)*. The octagonal shape will be cut by first tapering the stock to the dimensions of the first square you drew, then by planing the corners of that square down to the remaining sides of the second square. Extend the taper lines from the end to the start line *(above)*.

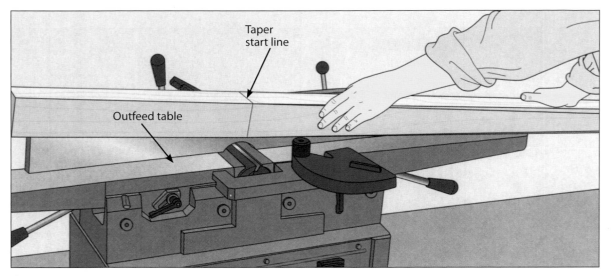

Taper
start line

Outfeed table

2 Setting up and starting the taper. An easy way to taper the posts is with a jointer. Set the machine for a shallow cut and position the fence to expose only about 4 inches of the cutterhead. For this operation, also adjust the guard out of the way. Then, holding the blank against the fence, align the taper start line with the front of the outfeed table. To start each pass, carefully lower the blank onto the cutterhead while holding it firmly against the fence *(above)*. Make sure both hands are over the infeed side of the table.

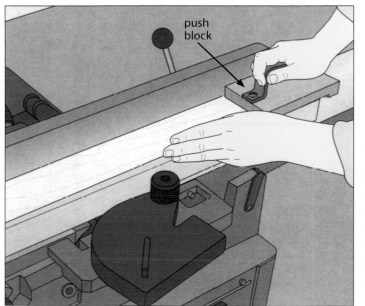

push block

3 Tapering the posts. Feed the leg across the cutterhead with a push block, pressing down on the trailing end of the stock while holding it flush against the fence *(left)*. Keep your left hand away from the cutterhead. Make as many passes as necessary until you have trimmed the stock to the taper outline, repeating the process to shape the remaining faces. If your markings are correct, you should make the same number of passes on each side. Clean up the taper at the start line using a belt sander.

Beveling Tapers

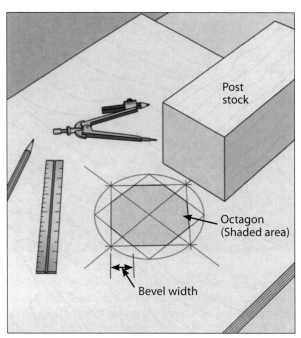

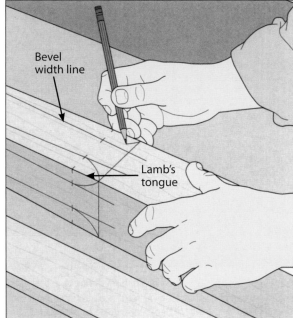

1 Laying out the bevels. To form the octagon, bevel the corners of the square taper. The bevel is already outlined on the end of each post, but it must also be marked on the sides of the stock. Taking the dimensions from a piece of full-size post stock, and drawing on scrap plywood, outline squares as you did in step 1 *(page 74)*. Transfer your measurement—equal to the bevel width—to the post, measuring from each corner of the square to either side. Then use a pencil and a long straightedge to connect each mark with its corresponding point on the octagon drawn at the top end of each post. Once all eight bevel lines are marked, draw a curved lamb's tongue at each corner, joining the bevel marks with the taper start line *(above, right)*.

2 Roughing out the bevels. To secure the posts, use three wood blocks. Cut V-shaped notches into an edge of each one, then place two of the blocks under the workpiece to support it and clamp one on top between the other two; position two of the blocks around the square portion of the post. Then use a drawknife to shape the tapered portion of the posts into octagons, beveling one corner at a time. Holding the drawknife on the stock bevel-side down, pull the tool toward the top end of the post *(right)*. The depth of cut depends on how much you tilt the handles; the lower the angle, the shallower the cut. Take a light shaving, always following the wood grain.

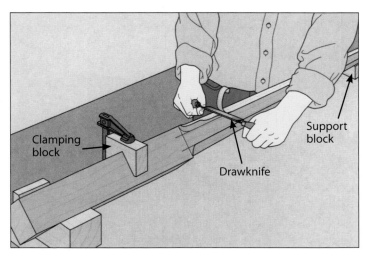

3 **Smoothing the bevels.** Once all the bevels have been cut, use a bench plane to flatten the eight sides of the posts' tapered section. Adjust the tool to a very light cut and work from the taper start line toward the post's top end to level the surface *(right)*. To avoid tearout, work with the wood grain. Reposition the post in the wood blocks as necessary to flatten the remaining sides.

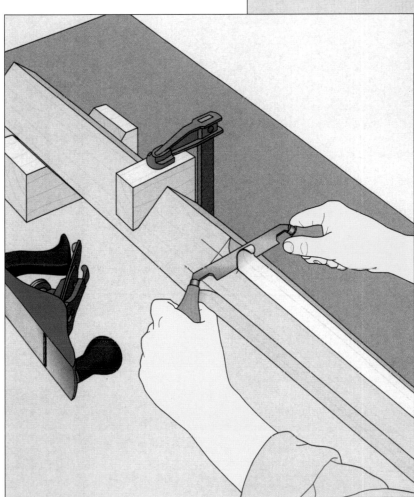

4 **Shaping the lamb's tongue.** To complete the pencil posts, switch back to the drawknife to bring the lamb's tongues to their final shape. Smooth out the transition between the tongues and the bevel lines *(left)*. Once you are finished draw-knifing, smooth the surface using a sanding block.

Anatomy of a Queen Anne Secretary

Desk Unit (*page 83*)

Top
Joined to sides with
half-blind dovetails.

Top of drawer section
Front edge is hinged to fall-front; ends
fit into groove in carcase sides.

Back Panel
Fits into rabbets cut along back
edges of carcase panels.

Dust frame (*page 86*)
Supports drawer. Assembled with plate
joints; side pieces fit into grooves in
carcase sides.

Drawer divider
Assembled and fixed
to dust frame below
with plate joints.

Loper (*page 89*)
Supports fall-front when in down position.
Dowel glued into inside face slides in slot
in loper housing; piece joined to front end
with sliding dovetail conceals end grain.

Side
Joined to
top and
bottom with
half-blind
dovetails.

Loper housing
Features slot that guides loper; top
edge fits into groove in underside
of drawer section top.

Leather inlay

Fall-front (*page 95*)
Hinged to top of
drawer section; serves
as writing surface in
down position. Outside
face is veneered;
inside face features
leather inlay.

Base
(*page 102*)

**Layered
base
molding**

Bottom
Joined to sides with
half-blind dovetails.

Bracket feet
Glued to
molding.

Drawer bottom
Fits into grooves in
front, back, and sides.

False front
Glued to
drawer front.

Front

Bookcase *(page 104)*

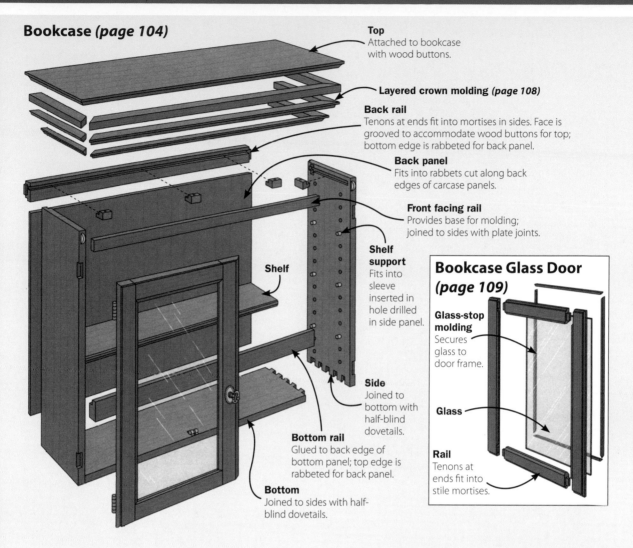

Top
Attached to bookcase with wood buttons.

Layered crown molding *(page 108)*

Back rail
Tenons at ends fit into mortises in sides. Face is grooved to accommodate wood buttons for top; bottom edge is rabbeted for back panel.

Back panel
Fits into rabbets cut along back edges of carcase panels.

Front facing rail
Provides base for molding; joined to sides with plate joints.

Shelf support
Fits into sleeve inserted in hole drilled in side panel.

Shelf

Bookcase Glass Door *(page 109)*

Glass-stop molding
Secures glass to door frame.

Glass

Rail
Tenons at ends fit into stile mortises.

Side
Joined to bottom with half-blind dovetails.

Bottom rail
Glued to back edge of bottom panel; top edge is rabbeted for back panel.

Bottom
Joined to sides with half-blind dovetails.

The major components of the Queen Anne secretary are shown in exploded form in this section. The desk unit is essentially a carcase with drawers, a fall-front, and an opening for the pigeonhole unit. All the corner joints are dovetailed. The drawers are supported by dust frames. To allow for wood movement as a result of changes in humidity, the frames are glued to the sides only near the front. The fall-front is fixed to the unit with butt hinges. To ease the strain on the hinges when the fall-front is let down, a pair of boards, called lopers, slide out to provide support.

The bookcase *(above)* is another solid-panel carcase with shelves, a back panel, and crown molding. The shelves are fully adjustable; they sit on pins that can be inserted at any height in the sides. The glass doors that grace the bookcase and protect its contents are hinged to the side panels. The pigeonhole unit is a smaller carcase with three drawers and a series of vertical dividers.

Pigeonhole Unit *(page 93)*

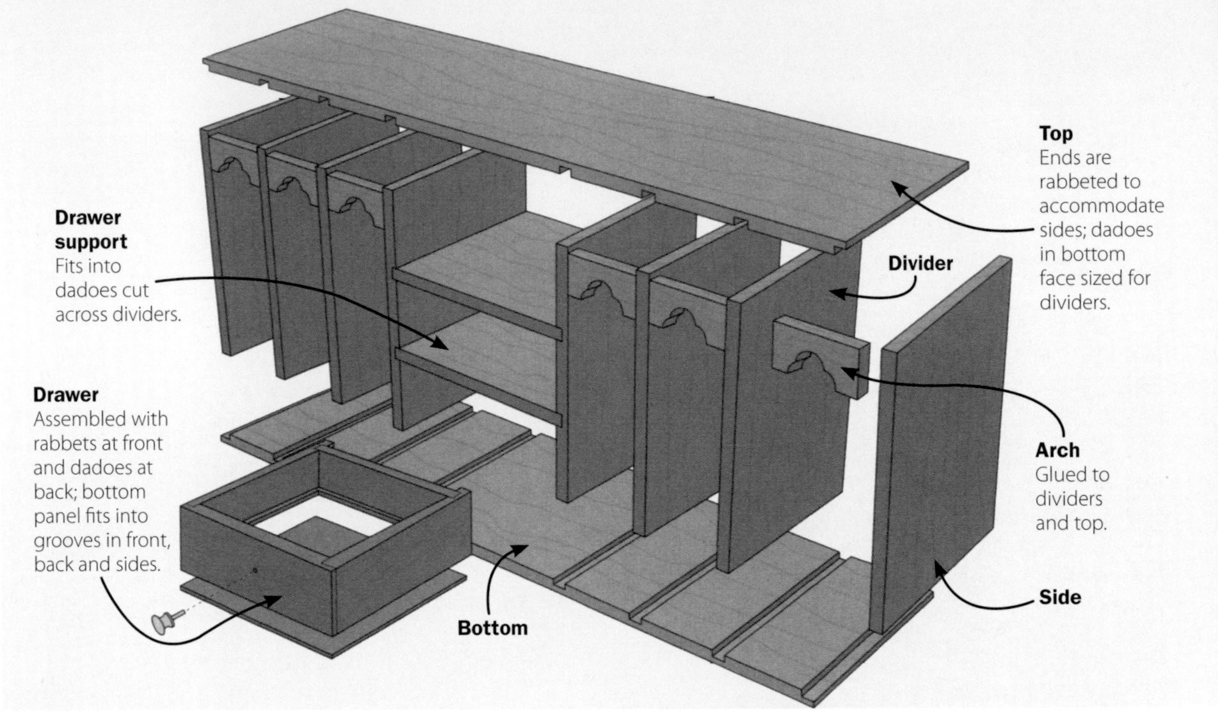
Top
Ends are rabbeted to accommodate sides; dadoes in bottom face sized for dividers.
Drawer support
Fits into dadoes cut across dividers.
Divider
Drawer
Assembled with rabbets at front and dadoes at back; bottom panel fits into grooves in front, back and sides.
Arch
Glued to dividers and top.
Side
Bottom

Cutting List (in inches)

	T	W	L		T	W	L		T	W	L
Bureau: Fall Front				1 Molding frame back	¾	2	30	2 Drawer supports	½	8½	9¼
1 Panel	⅜	10¼	29½	2 Molding frame sides	¾	2	17½	6 Arches	½	1½	3¼
2 Rails	¾	2¼	14	6 Bracket feet	¾	3	8	3 Drawer fronts	½	3	8½
2 Stiles	¾	2¼	33⅛	**Bureau: Deep Drawers**				3 Drawer backs	½	3	8
Bureau: Carcase				4 Upper front and back	¾	4 15/16	15¾	6 Drawer sides	½	3	8½
2 Sides	¾	17½	38	4 Upper sides	¾	4 15/16	17	3 Bottoms	½	8	8
1 Top	¾	10⅞	33⅛	2 Upper false fronts	¾	5	15⅞	**Bookcase: Carcase**			
1 Bottom	¾	17½	33⅛	2 Upper drawer bottoms	¼	15	16½	2 Sides	¾	8½	35¼
1 Back Panel	¼	32¾	37¼	2 Middle front and back	¾	5 15/16	32⅜	1 Top	¾	11¾	38
1 Writing surface	¾	17½	32½	2 Middle sides	¾	5 15/16	17	1 Bottom	¾	8½	32⅛
2 Lopers	¾	3¾	17	1 Middle false front	¾	6	32½	1 Front facing rail	¾	3¼	33
2 Loper housings	¾	3¾	17	2 Lower front and back	¾	6 15/16	32⅜	1 Back rail	¾	3	31½
6 Dust frame stiles	¾	2	32½	2 Lower sides	¾	6 15/16	17	1 Bottom Rail	¾	2	31½
6 Dust frame rails	¾	2	13¼	1 Lower false front	¾	7	33½	1 Molding frame front	¾	2	36½
1 Cross rail	¾	4	13¼	2 Drawer bottoms	¼	31½	16½	2 Molding frame sides	¾	2	11
1 Drawer divider	¾	2	15¼	**Bureau: Shallow Drawer**				1 Molding front (built up)	1¼	1¼	35¾
1 Muntin	¾	2	5	2 Front and back	¾	3 11/16	29⅛	2 Molding sides	1¼	1¼	10¾
Bureau: Base				2 Sides	¾	3 11/16	17	1 Back panel	¼	29½	32¾
1 Molding front	¾	⅞	35¾	1 False front	¾	3¾	29¼	**Bookcase: Doors**			
2 Molding sides	¾	⅞	18⅜	1 Drawer bottom	¼	28⅜	16½	4 Stiles	¾	2	31¾
1 Molding base front	¾	3	35¾	**Bureau: Pigeonhole Unit**				4 Rails	¾	2	12½
2 Molding base sides	¾	3	19⅛	2 Top and bottom	½	8½	32½	1 Glass-stop molding	¼	¼	192
1 Molding frame front	¾	2	34	8 Dividers and sides	½	8½	10½	2 Glass panes	⅛	12 5/16	27⅝

Making the Desk Unit

The carcases of the desk unit and bookcase form the two main parts of the secretary. In keeping with the twin requirements of elegance and usefulness, both pieces are assembled with the half-blind dovetail. The steps shown on the following pages feature the connection between the top and sides of the desk unit; but the same procedures apply to the joints at the bottom of the both the desk and bookcase units.

Once the dovetails have been cut, you can move on to making the dust frames *(page 86)* and the loper housings. The carcase is then assembled *(page 87)* and the back panel is nailed in place *(page 89)*. The final step, once the glue has cured, is installing the lopers.

A plate joiner cuts a slot in the stile of a dust frame; a stop block clamped in place holds the workpiece square to the tool. A wood biscuit and glue will be added to the semicircular cut and then fitted into a mating slot in a rail. Quick and easy to make, the resulting joint will be strong and invisible, enabling the frame to support a drawer.

Cutting Half-Blind Dovetails

Dovetail square

Tail-end line

Half-pin

Side of desk unit

Shoulder line

1 Marking the pins in the sides. Once you have glued up the panels and cut them to the right size, mark their outside faces with an X. Secure one of the side panels upright in a vise, then set a cutting gauge to about two-thirds the thickness of the sides and mark a line across the end to indicate the end of the tails. The line should be closer to the outside than the inside face of the panel. Adjust the cutting gauge to the stock thickness and scribe a line on the inside face of the side to mark the shoulder line of the tails. Next, use a dovetail square to outline the pins on the ends of the side; the wide part of the pins should be on the inside face of the panel *(left)*. There are no strict guidelines for spacing dovetail pins, but for stock of the dimensions provided on page 82, 1¼-inch evenly spaced pins with ⅝-inch tails and a half-pin at each edge will make for a strong and attractive joint. To complete the marking, extend the lines on the panel end to the shoulder line on its inside face. Mark the waste sections with Xs as you go.

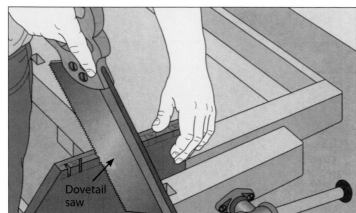

Dovetail saw

2 Cutting the pins. Leaving the side panel in the vise, cut along the edges of the pins with a dovetail saw *(left)*, working your way from one panel edge to the other. (Some woodworkers prefer to cut all the right-hand edges first, then all the left-hand edges.) Hold the panel steady and align the saw blade just to the waste side of the cutting line; angle the saw toward the waste to avoid cutting into the pins. Use smooth, even strokes, allowing the saw to cut on the push stroke. Continue the cut just to the shoulder line, then repeat to saw the pins at the other end of the panel.

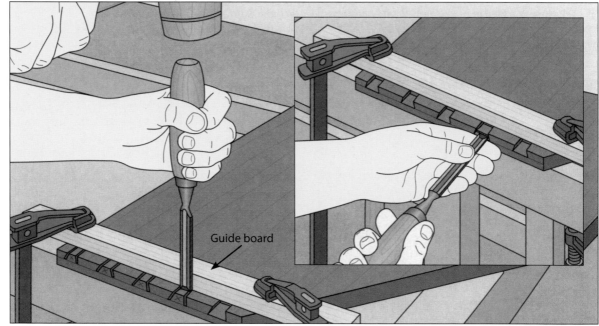

Guide board

3 Chiseling out the waste. Set the panel inside-face up on a work suface and clamp a guide board to it, aligning its edge with the waste side of the shoulder line. Starting at one edge of the stock, hold the flat side of a chisel against the guide block; the blade should be no wider than the narrowest part of the waste section. With the chisel perpendicular to the face of the board, strike the handle with a wooden mallet, making a ⅛-inch-deep cut into the waste *(above)*. Then hold the chisel bevel up and square to the end of the board about ⅛ inch below the top surface and peel away a thin layer of waste. Continue until you reach the scribed line on the end of the board, then repeat the process with the remaining waste sections. Pare away any excess waste from between the pins, completing work on one waste section before moving to the next. Press the flat side of the chisel against the bottom of the section with the thumb of your left hand; with your right hand, push the chisel toward the shoulder line, shaving away the last slivers of waste *(inset)*. Then pare away any waste from the sides of the pins.

4 Laying out the tails. Set the top panel outside-face down on the work surface and scribe a shoulder line the thickness of the stock from the end of the workpiece. Secure a side panel in a handscrew, then hold the panel top-end down with its inside face aligned with the line on the top panel. Making certain that the straight edges of the boards are flush, clamp the handscrew to the bench. Outline the tails with a pencil *(right)*, then extend the lines on the panel end using a try square. Mark all the waste section with Xs.

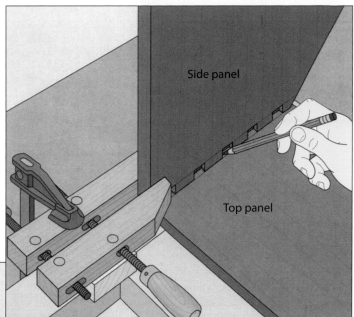

Side panel

Top panel

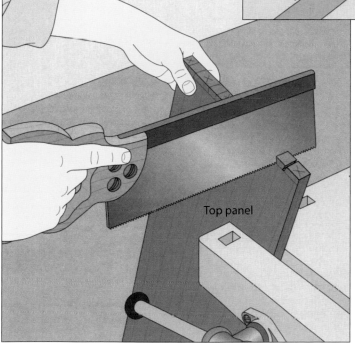

Top panel

5 Cutting the tails. Use a dovetail saw to cut the tails the same way you sawed the pins. Angling the board, as shown at left, rather than the saw, makes for easier, more accurate, cutting. Secure the panel so the right-hand edges of the tails are vertical. Saw smoothly and evenly along the edges of the tails, stopping at the shoulder line. Reposition the panel in the vise to cut the left-hand edges. Once all the saw cuts have been made, remove the waste with a chisel. To avoid splitting the tails, remove about half the waste, then turn the panel over to chisel out the remaining waste.

Making the Dust Frames

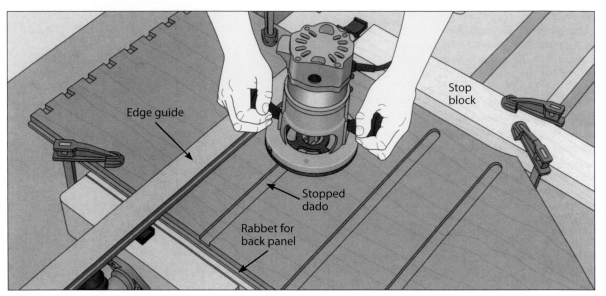

Edge guide

Stop block

Stopped dado

Rabbet for back panel

1 Dadoing the carcase sides. Use a router to cut ⅜-inch-wide, 3/16-inch-deep rabbets around the back edge of the carcase to accommodate the back. Then prepare the sides for the dust frames. The ends of the frames fit into stopped dadoes in the sides. To cut the dadoes, install a ¾-inch straight bit in your router, set the cutting depth to ¼ inch, and secure one of the side panels inside-face up to a work surface. Refer to the anatomy illustration and the drawer measurements on page 82 to outline the dadoes on the stock, then clamp an edge guide to the panel so the bit will be centered on the first marked line. Also clamp a stop block along the front edge of the panel so the dado will stop 2 inches short of the edge. For each dust frame, rout a stopped dado from the back edge of the side panel *(above)*, stopping when the router base plate contacts the stop block. Square the ends of the dado with a chisel.

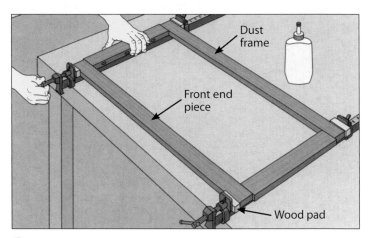

Dust frame

Front end piece

Wood pad

2 Making and gluing up the dust frames. Cut the pieces of the dust frames to length and drill elongated screw holes in the end boards; to allow for wood movement, the holes should be longer and wider than the shanks of the fasteners you will use to attach the frames to the carcase sides. Sand any frame surfaces that will be difficult to reach after glue up. Cut a plate joint at each corner of the frames, assemble the joints with wood biscuits and glue, then secure them with bar clamps, aligning the bars with the end pieces and protecting the stock with wood pads *(above)*. Make sure the front end piece is recessed by an amount equal to the depth of the dadoes you cut in step 1. When making the dust frame for the two narrower drawers, include the cross rail *(page 80)*.

Assembling the Carcase

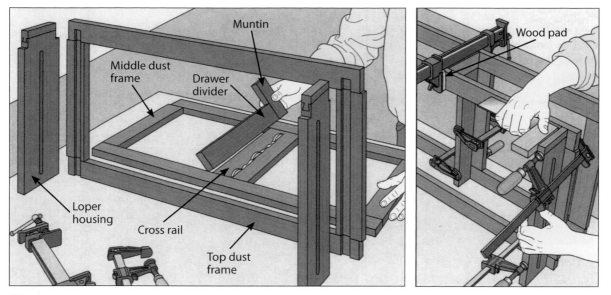

1 Installing the drawer divider and loper housings. Cut the loper housings to size *(page 89)*, using a sliding dovetail to add a piece to the front end of each one to hide the end grain. Then rout the ¼-inch-wide slots in the housings for the loper dowels. Make the L-shaped drawer divider and attach it to the cross rail of the middle dust frame with a biscuit joint *(above, left)*. Cut another biscuit slot into the muntin and a matching slot in the top dust frame above it. Next, rout grooves into the underside of the top panel and top face of the uppermost dust frame to accommodate the loper housings. Spread glue in the slots and grooves, then fit the dust frames together, using clamps to secure the drawer divider, the loper housings, and the frames in place. Protect the stock with wood pads and use a try square to check that the assembly is square *(above, right)*.

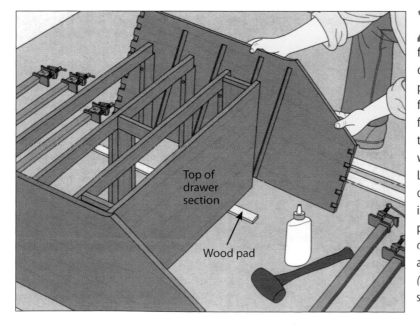

2 Fitting the sides and dust frames together. Working on the shop floor, spread glue along the entire length of the side panel dadoes for the top panel of the drawer unit, but only in the front 2 inches of the dadoes for the dust frames. To allow for wood movement, the remaining length of the dust frames will be attached to the sides with screws. Laying one side panel outside-face down on long wood pads, fit the dust frames into their dadoes and screw them in place. Fit the top panel into its dado, carefully turn the assembly onto its back, and set the other side panel in position *(left)*. Drive the remaining screws to secure the dust frames and side panel.

Making the Drawers

The desk unit drawers are assembled with through dovetails, then a false front is glued to the drawer front to conceal the end grain of the tails. The chamfer cut around the perimeter of the false front shown above recalls the traditional practice of beveling the ends and edges of veneered drawer fronts, which prevented the veneer from being torn off when the drawer was opened and closed.

Gluing up the Drawers

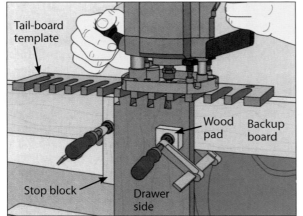

Tail-board template

Wood pad

Backup board

Stop block

Drawer side

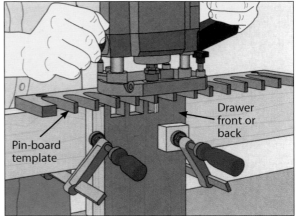

Pin-board template

Drawer front or back

1 Routing the through dovetail joints. Size the drawer parts to fit their openings in the desk unit, then join the boards with dovetails, cutting the pins in the front and back of the drawer, and the tails in the sides. To cut the dovetails with a router and the jig shown above, screw the pin- and tail-board templates to backup boards, then secure one of the tail boards (drawer sides) end up in a bench vise. Protecting the stock with a wood pad, clamp the tail template to the work-piece so the underside of the template is butted against the end of the board. Also clamp a stop block against one edge of the drawer side so the tails at the other end and

in the other drawer sides will match. Install a top-piloted dovetail bit in the router and cut the tails by feeding the tool along the top of the template and moving the bit in and out of the jig's slots *(above, left)*. Keep the bit pilot pressed against the sides of the slot throughout. Repeat to rout the tails at the other end of the board and in the other drawer sides. Then use the completed tails to outline the pins on the drawer fronts and backs. Secure a pin board in the vise, clamp the pin-board template to the board with the slots aligned over the outline, and secure the stop block in place. Rout the pins with a straight bit *(above, right)*.

2 Preparing the drawers for bottom panels.

The bottom of each desk unit drawer fits into a groove along the inside of the drawer. Dry-fit the parts together, then clamp the unit securely, protecting the stock with wood pads and aligning the clamp bars with the front and back. Fit a router with a piloted three-wing slotting cutter and mount the tool in a table. Adjust the bit height to cut the groove ¼ inch from the drawer's bottom edge. Set the drawer right side up on the table and, starting at the middle of one side, feed the stock into the cutter against the direction of bit rotation. Keeping the pilot bearing butted against the workpiece, feed the drawer clockwise *(right)*. Continue pivoting the drawer on the table until you return to the starting point. Use veneered plywood for the bottom and cut the panel to fit the opening.

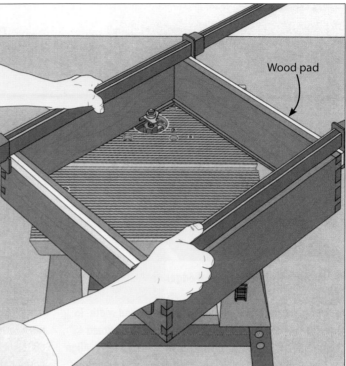

Wood pad

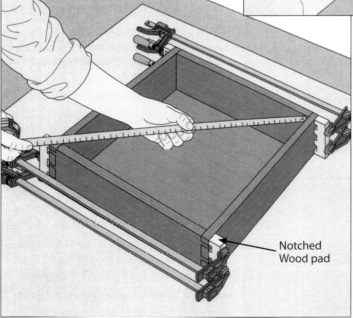

Notched Wood pad

3 Gluing and clamping the drawers. For

glue up, make four wood pads as long as the height of the drawers and cut small notches in the pads so they only contact the tails. Spread a thin, even layer of glue on all the contacting surfaces, then assemble the drawers and install two bar clamps across the pin boards. Tighten the clamps a little at a time until a small amount of glue squeezes out of the joints. Immediately measure the diagonals between opposite corners *(left)*. The two results should be the same. If not, install another bar clamp across the longer of the two diagonals, setting the clamp jaws on those already in place. Tighten the clamp a little at a time, measuring as you go until the two diagonals are equal.

2 Preparing the frame for the panel.

The fall-front panel sits in a groove cut around the inside edges of the frame. Install a piloted three-wing slotting cutter in the router and align the fence with the bit's pilot bearing. Adjust the bit height so the top edge of the cutter is centered on the edge of the stock. Since the groove will have to accommodate both the panel and the veneer glued to it, you will need at least two passes to rout a sufficiently wide groove. Feed the stock as in step 1, riding the unchamfered edge along the fence; finish the pass with a push stick. Then turn over the workpiece and repeat to widen the groove *(right)*. Now, cut the four frame pieces to length, mitering the ends. Once the veneered panel is ready, the frame will be assembled using plate joints. (The finished frame, along with the veneered panel, is shown on page 80.)

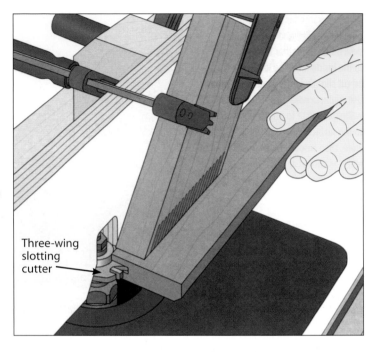

Three-wing slotting cutter

A Variety of Veneered Panels

Slip match
Often used to dramatic effect; reduces distortion caused by light refraction problems when book-matching.

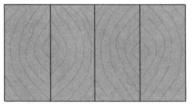

Book match
A repeating pattern in which adjoining sheets of veneer appear to radiate from the joint between them, like the pages of an open book.

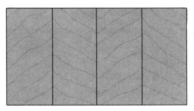

Herringbone
Veneer figure runs diagonally off each sheet, creating a zigzag effect.

End-to-end
A mirror-image pattern featuring flat-cut veneers with prominent landscape figure.

Butt-and-book match
Commonly used with butt, crotch, and stump veneers to create an unfolding, circular effect.

Reverse-diamond match
Features four sheets of veneer that appear to converge at the center.

Making the Veneered Panel

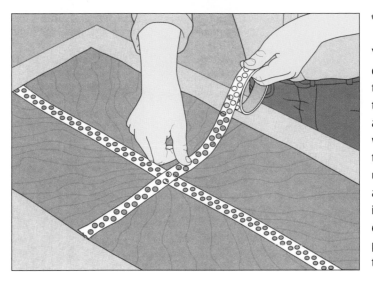

1 **Creating the veneer pattern.** Cover the outside face of the full-front panel with veneer. You can buy ready-matched sheets and glue them down as-is or make your own match, referring to one of the patterns illustrated on page 96; the secretary featured in this chapter uses a butt-and-book match. To apply more than one sheet of veneer to a panel face with a veneer press *(page 99)*, tape the sheets together and glue them down as a unit. Start by aligning the sheets edge to edge on a work surface, good-side up, to produce a visually interesting pattern. The combined length and width of the veneer should equal the dimensions of the panel. Once you have a satisfactory arrangement, tape the sheets together using veneer tape *(left)*.

2 **Setting up a vacuum press.** Featuring a sealed vacuum bag and a 5-cfm (cubic feet per minute) vacuum pump, the press shown in step 3 can exert pressure greater than 1,000 pounds per square foot. The press works by withdrawing most of the air from the bag; the resulting outside air pressure secures the veneer. To set up the press, cut the platen and caul to the same size as your substrate panel *(right)*. The platen should be made from medium-density fiberboard or particleboard at least ¾ inch thick. Cut the caul from any type of manufactured board (other than plywood) at least ½ inch thick. To prepare the platen, round over its corners to avoid tearing the bag, then cut a grid of grooves ⅛ inch deep and wide across its surface, spaced 4 to 6 inches apart. Finally, bore a ⅝-inch hole 2 inches from one end of the platen and centered between its edges. Slip the sleeve supplied with the press into the hole. The sleeve will ensure a tight connection with the vacuum hose.

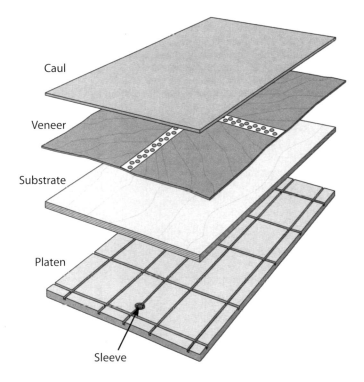

Caul

Veneer

Substrate

Platen

Sleeve

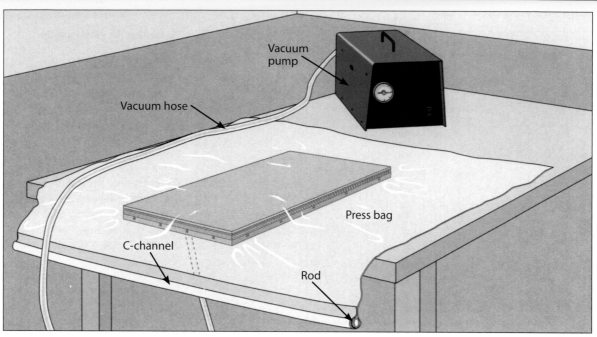

3 Veneering the panel. Use the vacuum press to glue the veneer down to the panel, following the manufacturer's instructions. For the model shown, insert the hose into the nipple in the bottom of the press bag. Then place the platen in the bag and slide the nipple into the platen sleeve. Set the substrate panel on a work surface, apply the glue, and lay the veneer tape-side up on the substrate. Place a piece of wax paper over the veneer, rest the caul on top, and place the assembly atop the platen. Seal the bag, turn on the pump, and leave the assembly under pressure for the recommended length of time *(above)*. Most vacuum presses will automatically shut off when the appropriate pressure has been reached.

4 Assembling the fall-front. Once the veneer has been secured, remove the tape and gently sand surfaces that will be difficult to reach after the frame is glued together. Ready the frame pieces for plate joints, applying the glue and wood biscuits at the mitered end of the boards. Do not insert any adhesive in the panel grooves; the panel must be free to move. To prevent the wood biscuits from expanding before everything is put together, assemble the frame as quickly as possible, fitting the frames pieces to the panel *(right)*. With wood pads protecting the frame, secure the plate joints with bar clamps.

Veneer Press

Made from plywood, hardwood, and six 9-inch-long press screws, the inexpensive shop-built veneer press shown below will work as well as a commercial model. The dimensions provided in the illustration will yield a press capable of veneering panels up to 16 by 29½ inches.

Start by cutting the rails and stiles from hardwood. Bore three equidistant holes through the middle of each top rail, sized slightly larger than the diameter of the press screw collars you will be using. Next, join the rails and stiles into two rectangular frames. The press in the illustration is assembled with open mortise-and-tenon joints *(inset)*, but through dovetails can also be used. Whichever joinery method you use, reinforce each joint with glue and three screws.

Now cut the pieces for the base and caul to size. Both are made from two pieces of ¾-inch plywood face-glued and screwed together. To assemble the press, set the two frames on their sides on a work surface and screw the base to the bottom rails, driving the fasteners from the bottom of the rails. Attach the press screws to the top rails by removing the swivel heads and collars, then tapping the collars into the holes in the top rails from underneath. Slip the threaded sections into the collars and reattach them to the swivel heads.

To use the press, apply the glue and lay the veneer tape-side up on the substrate. Set the panel on the base of the press, veneered-face down with a strip of wax paper between the veneer and the base. Starting in the middle of the panel to prevent adhesive from becoming trapped, tighten the press clamps one at a time until a thin glue bead squeezes out from under the panel.

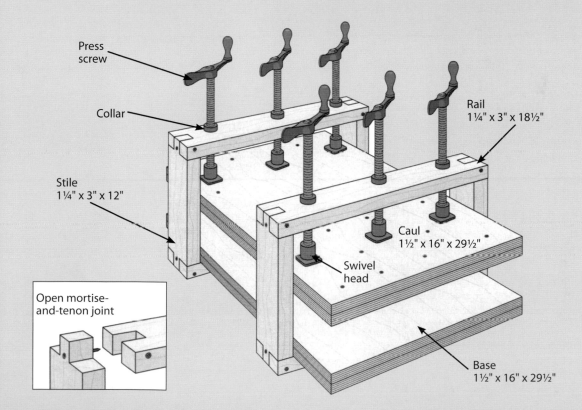

Press screw

Collar

Stile
1¼" x 3" x 12"

Rail
1¼" x 3" x 18½"

Caul
1½" x 16" x 29½"

Swivel head

Open mortise-and-tenon joint

Base
1½" x 16" x 29½"

Attaching the Fall-Front to the Desk Unit

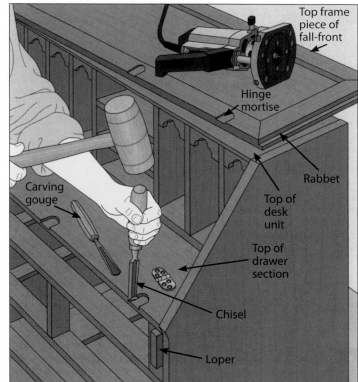

Top frame piece of fall-front

Hinge mortise

Rabbet

Top of desk unit

Top of drawer section

Carving gouge

Chisel

Loper

1 **Making the hinge mortises.** Use your table saw to cut a ⅜-inch wide rabbet along the sides of the frame. Begin with a shallow depth of cut, increasing the depth by ⅛ inch with each pass until the fall-front's bottom edge is 1⁄16 inch above the top of the drawer unit when the fall-front is in position. Once you are satisfied with the fit, lay the fall-front veneer-face down on the lopers and butt the bottom edge against the top of the drawer section. Position and outline the three hinges on the pieces—one in the middle and one each near the sides—centering the hinge pin on the seam between the fall-front and the carcase. To cut the hinge mortises, install a ⅛-inch straight bit in your router, set the cutting depth to the hinge leaf thickness, and cut out the waste inside the outline. Use a chisel, a carving gouge, and a wooden mallet to pare to the line *(left)*. Test-fit the hinges in their mortises and use the chisel to deepen or widen any of the recesses, if necessary.

2 **Attaching the fall-front to the desk unit.** Set the hinges in their mortises in the desk unit and mark the screw holes, then drill pilot holes and screw the hinge leaves in place, leaving the fasteners a little loose. Mark the drilling depth on the drill bit by wrapping a strip of masking tape around it. Next, extend the lopers and set the fall-front in position, slipping the free hinge leaves into their mortises. Mark the screw holes, drill pilot holes, and screw the hinges to the fall-front, then finish tightening all the screws *(right)*. If you are using brass screws, be careful not to overtighten them or they will break. It is a good idea to drive in a standard wood screw first to tap the pilot hole.

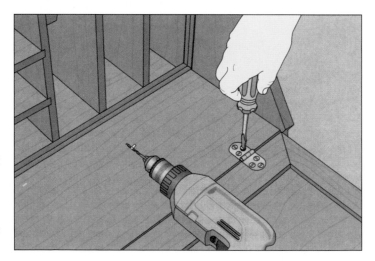

Installing the Fall-Front Lock

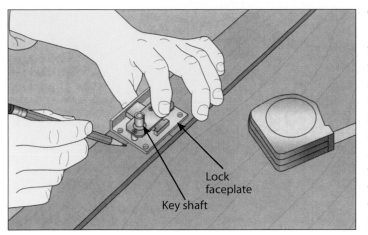

Lock faceplate

Key shaft

1 Outlining the lock faceplate. Open the fall-front to its down position and place the lock face down on the top frame piece so the key shaft will be centered between the sides; the lock should also be flush with the top edge of the panel. If the key shaft is off-center, as is the case with the lock shown, you will need to use a tape measure and a try square to mark the middle of the fall-front and align the key shaft with it *(left)*. Drill the hole for the key shaft and insert the shaft through the hole. Once the lock is properly positioned, trace the outline of the lock faceplate, then extend the lines onto the top edge of the fall-front.

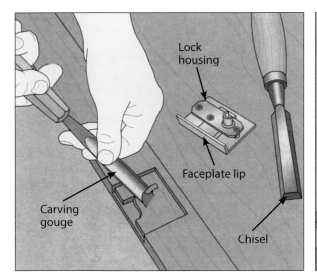

Lock housing

Faceplate lip

Carving gouge

Chisel

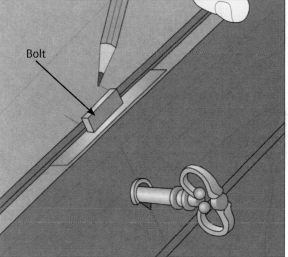

Bolt

2 Routing the lock mortise. Start by using a chisel to cut a shallow mortise for the faceplate lip in the top edge of the fall-front. Next, install a straight bit in your router, set the cutting depth to the faceplate thickness, and cut a mortise within the marked outline. Use the chisel to square the corners and pare to the line. To cut the mortise for the lock housing, measure the distance between the edges of the faceplate and the housing, and transfer your measurement to the mortise. Then use a carving gouge to cut the final mortise *(above)*. Test-fit the lock in the cavity and use the chisel or gouge to deepen or widen any of the mortises, if necessary. Finally, screw the lock in place.

3 Installing the strike plate. Fit the key into the lock. To locate the strike plate for the bolt, turn the key to extend the bolt and use a pencil to coat the end of the bolt with graphite. Retract the bolt and swing the fall-front to the closed position. Extend the bolt against the underside of the carcase top to mark its location. Also extend the bolt against the edge of the top panel and mark its sides on the top *(above)*. Position the strike plate on the carcase top, centering its opening on the pencil marks. Outline the plate, then cut a shallow recess for it and a deeper mortise for the bolt. Finally, mark the plate's screw holes, bore a pilot hole at each mark, and fasten the plate in position.

The bottom of the secretary's desk unit sits on a base supported by bracket feet at each corner. The bottom edges of the carcase are concealed by molding, which is attached to the base, but not glued to the carcase. This allows the panels of the desk unit to move with changes in humidity without damaging the molding.

Making and Installing the Base

Anatomy of the Desk Unit Base

Back rail

Molding frame

Molding

Side rail

Front rail

Molding base

Bracket feet

1 **Routing the molding.** Cut a board longer and wider than you will need for the three pieces of molding. Install a Roman ogee bit *(inset)* in your router and mount the tool in a table. Align the bit's pilot bearing with the fence and adjust the cutting height to leave a flat lip no more than ¼ inch thick on the edge of the stock above the molding. Mount two featherboards on the fence and one on the table to secure the workpiece. (In this illustration, the featherboard on the outfeed side of the fence has been removed for clarity.) Turn on the tool and feed the stock *(right)*. To complete the pass, move to the outfeed side of the table and pull the stock through the end of the cut. Make several passes, increasing the width of cut ⅛ inch at a time. Rip the molding strips from the board on your table saw, then cut them to length, mitering both ends of the front piece and the front end of the side pieces.

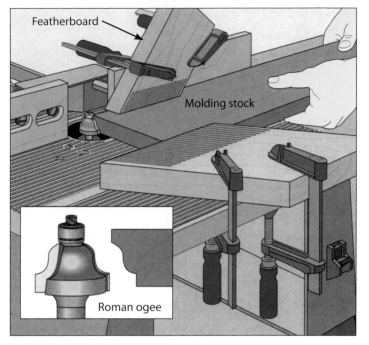

Featherboard

Molding stock

Roman ogee

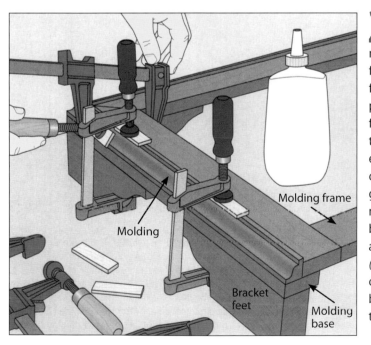

Molding

Molding frame

Bracket feet

Molding base

2 **Gluing up the base.** Cut the rails of the molding frame and molding base to length, mitering both ends of the front pieces and the front end of the side pieces; omit the back rail for the base. Join the corners of the frames with plate joints and clamp them as you did the dust frames *(page 86)*. Next, glue the molding base to the underside of the frame so the sides of the base extend beyond the frame by about 1 inch. Then cut the bracket feet on your band saw. Spread glue on the contacting surfaces between the molding pieces, the bracket feet, and the molding base, then fit the pieces together and clamp the assembly, protecting the stock with wood pads *(left)*. Once the adhesive has cured, remove the clamps and attach the base to the desk unit by screwing the molding frame to the carcase through elongated screw holes.

Making the Bookcase

Adjustable shelves give the bookcase section of the secretary greater flexibility, enabling you to adapt to changing needs and organize space most efficiently. The solid brass shelf supports shown at right can be slipped into any of the sleeves along the side panels, permitting the shelves to be mounted at any height in the bookcase.

Preparing the Side Panels for Adjustable Shelving

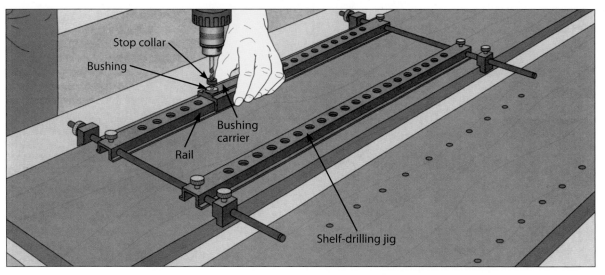

Stop collar

Bushing

Bushing carrier

Rail

Shelf-drilling jig

1 Drilling holes for shelf supports. Cut the side panels of the bookcase to width and length, then set them inside-face up on a work surface. The commercial jig shown above enables you to bore two parallel rows of holes in the side panels at 1-inch intervals and ensures that corresponding holes will be perfectly aligned. Clamp the jig to the edges of one panel; the holes can be any distance from the panel edges, but about 2 inches in would be best for the secretary. Fit an electric drill with a bit the same diameter as the sleeves and install a stop collar to mark the drilling depth equal to the sleeve length. Starting at either end of one of the jig's rails, place the appropriate bushing in the first hole of the bushing carrier. (The bushing keeps the bit perfectly square to the workpiece.) Holding the drill and carrier, bore the hole. Drill a series of evenly spaced holes along both rails. Remove the jig and repeat for the other side panel, carefully positioning the jig so that the holes will be aligned with those in the first panel.

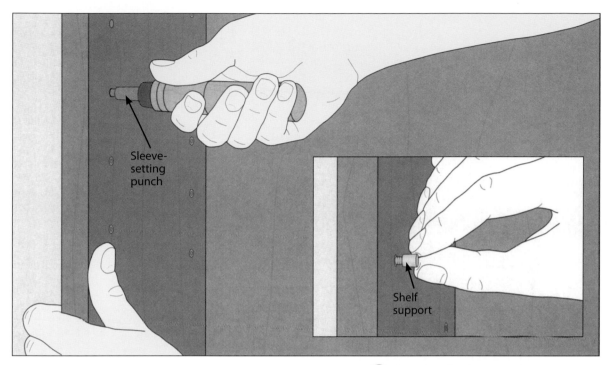

Sleeve-
setting
punch

Shelf
support

2 **Mounting the sleeves and supports.** To install the sleeves without damaging them, use a sleeve-setting punch. Place a sleeve on the end of the punch and push it firmly into one of the holes in a side panel *(above)*. Insert a sleeve into each hole you drilled. Once you have installed all the sleeves, insert shelf supports into the sleeves at each shelf location *(inset)*.

Shop Tip

A shop-made shelf-drilling jig
The T-shaped jig shown here
will enable you to drill a row
of evenly spaced holes as
accurately as with a commercial
jig. Make the jig from 1-by-3 stock,
being careful to screw the fence and
arm together at a perfect 90° angle.
Mark a line down the middle of the arm
and drill holes at 2-inch intervals along it
with the same bit you would use for the
sleeves. To use the jig, clamp it to the
side panel with the fence butted against
either end of the panel and the marked
centerline 2 inches in from its edge. Fit
your drill bit with a stop collar, bore the
holes, and reposition the jig for each
new row.

Assembling the Carcase

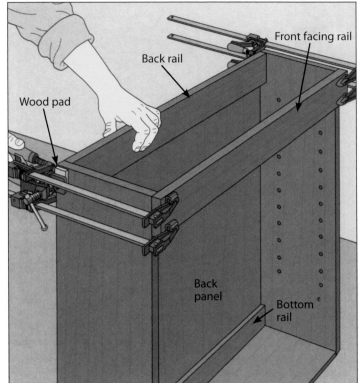

Back rail

Front facing rail

Wood pad

Back panel

Bottom rail

1 Gluing up the sides, bottom, and rails. Cut the remaining pieces of the bookcase carcase to size—the bottom, the rails, and the back panel. Next, saw a rabbet along the back edges of the sides and bottom for the back panel. Cut blind tenons at both ends of the back rail and drill a matching mortise on the inside face of each side panel. With a plate joiner, make slots for biscuits in the front and bottom rails, and mating ones in the sides. Use half-blind dovetails to join the sides to the bottom of the bookcase, cutting the pins in the sides and the tails in the bottom. Then spread glue on the contacting surfaces of all the pieces, inserting wood biscuits where appropriate, and fit them together. Protecting the stock with wood pads, install two bar clamps across each side, positioning the clamp jaws on the front and back rails, then install two more clamps across the back and bottom rails. Tighten the clamps evenly *(left)* until a thin glue bead squeezes out of the joints. Finally, nail the back panel in place.

2 Routing a groove for the top panel. To attach the top panel to the bookcase using wood buttons, as shown in this section, you will need to rout a groove for the buttons along the top of the carcase. Fit your router with a piloted three-wing slotting cutter and set the tool's cutting depth to locate the groove about ½ inch below the top edge of the carcase. Starting near one corner, guide the router along the top edge *(right)*. Move the tool in a clockwise direction, keeping the base plate flat and the bit's pilot bearing pressed against the stock.

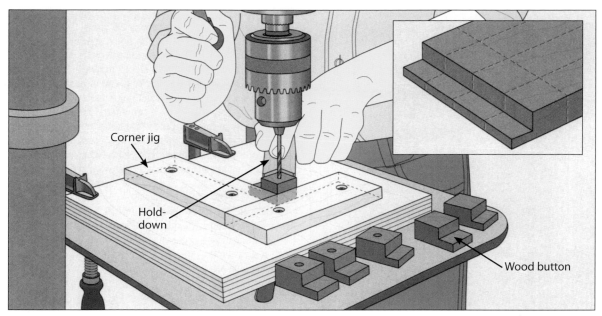

3 **Making the buttons.** You will need to place a wood button every 6 inches along the top edge of the carcase. Cut several 1-by-1¾-inch buttons from a single board; make the thickness of the stock equal to the gap between the bottom of the groove and the top edge of the carcase, less ⅟₁₆ inch. Cut a rabbet to fit the groove at each end of the board, then rip the board into 1-inch strips on your band saw and cut off the buttons about 1¾ inches from the ends *(inset)*. To make holes in the buttons for installation, use an L-shaped corner jig fashioned from a scrap of ¾-inch plywood and two pieces of wood. Clamp the jig to your drill press table and steady the buttons with a hold-down made from scrap wood. Drill through the centers on the unrabbeted portions of the buttons *(above)*.

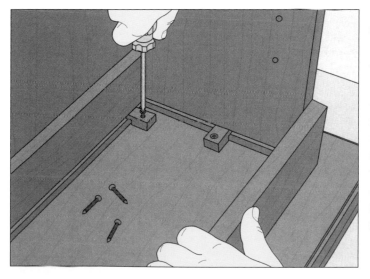

4 **Attaching the top.** Cut the bookcase top to size, then shape its ends and edges on a router table, using a decorative molding bit. Set the top outside-face down on a work surface and position the carcase on top. Fit the rabbeted end of a wood button into the groove in one of the side panels and insert another into the groove in the back rail about 6 inches away. Drill a pilot hole through the hole in the button and into the top, then screw the buttons in place *(left)*, leaving a ⅛-inch gap between the lipped ends of the buttons and the bottom of the groove. Install the remaining buttons, spacing them every 6 inches.

Making and Installing Crown Molding

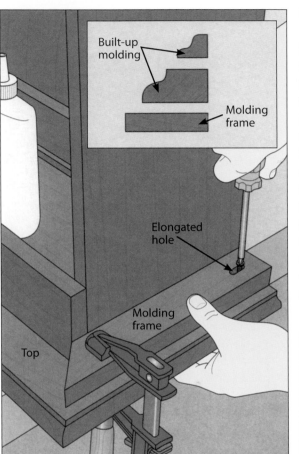

Built-up molding

Molding frame

Elongated hole

Molding frame

Top

1 Making the molding and attaching the frame. Fixed to the underside of the bookcase top and flush against the carcase, the crown molding consists of three layers *(inset)*. Cut the molding frame pieces to length, mitering both ends of the front piece and the front end of each side piece. Create the built-up molding on the router table as you did the base molding *(page 103)*, using two different ogee bits for the narrow and wider pieces. Cut the molding to length, mitering the pieces as you did the frame. Start by installing the molding frame. For the side pieces, drill an elongated hole through each board near the straight end; to allow for wood movement, spread glue on only the first 2 inches of the top face at the mitered end. Now, set the bookcase top-down on a work surface and position one side piece on the underside of the top. Install a bar clamp to secure the mitered end and drive a wood screw through the elongated hole and into the top to fix the back end *(left)*. Repeat for the other side, then install the front piece spreading glue along its entire length.

2 Applying the molding. The crown molding is fastened to the bookcase in two steps: The wider strips are attached first, followed by the narrower pieces on top. Spread a thin layer of glue on the bottom face of the wider strips, taking care not to get any glue on the edges since the molding should only be fixed to the molding frame, and not to the carcase. Set the strips on the molding frame, edges flush against the bookcase, making sure that the mitered ends butt together cleanly before clamping the molding in place. Once the adhesive has cured, remove the clamps and repeat the process for the narrower molding strips *(right)*. Cutting wood pads with convex curves matching the concave profile of the molding will not only protect the stock, but also help distribute clamping pressure evenly.

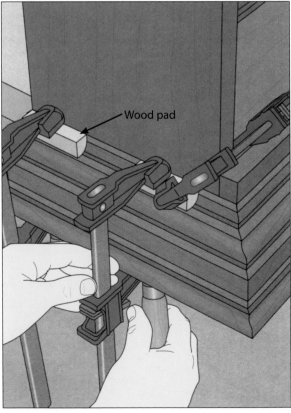

Wood pad

Making the Doors

An escutcheon is fastened to one of the doors of the bookcase shown at right. On this piece, the key and escutcheons are purely decorative. The doors are actually held shut by spring-loaded catches installed on the inside faces of the stiles near the bottom of the doors.

Making Frame-and-Panel Doors

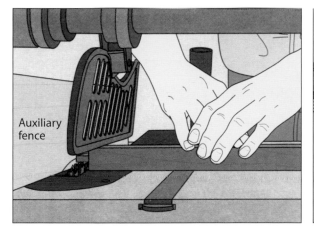

Auxiliary fence

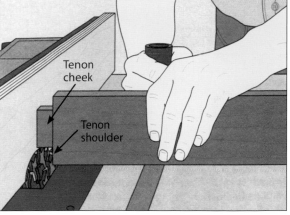

Tenon cheek

Tenon shoulder

1 Cutting the tenon in the rails. Start making the frame-and-panel doors of the bookcase by cutting blind tenons at the ends of all the rails. To do the job on your table saw, install a dado head slightly wider than the tenon length. Attach an auxiliary wood fence and notch it by raising the dado head into it. Set the width of cut equal to the tenon length and adjust the cutting height to about one-third the thickness of the stock. Holding the rail flush against the miter gauge and the fence, feed the stock facedown into the blades to cut one tenon cheek. Turn the board over and make the

same cut on the other side. Check for fit in a test mortise (step 4), then repeat the process on the other end of the board and on the other rails (above, left). To cut the tenon shoulders, set the cutting height at about ½ inch. Then, with the rail face flush against the miter gauge and the end butted against the fence, feed the workpiece into the blades. Turn the rail over and repeat the cut on the other side (above, right). Cut the rest of the tenon shoulders the same way. Fashion integrated molding on the inside edges of the door frames on a router table (page 103) using a piloted molding bit.

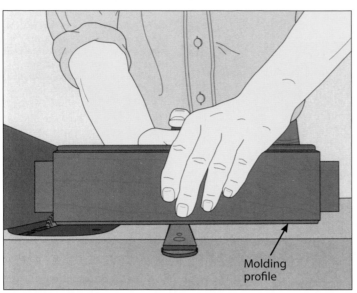

2 Preparing the rails for glue up. The corners of the tenon shoulders must be mitered to mate properly with the stiles. Remove the auxiliary fence from the table saw fence and install a crosscut or combination blade. Set the blade angle to 45°, make a test cut in a scrap board, and check the result with a combination square. Adjust the fence position and blade height so the cut is as wide and deep as the width of the edge molding. (The blade teeth should just protrude beyond the tenon shoulder.) To make the cuts, hold the piece flush against the fence and miter gauge as you feed it edge down into the blade. Repeat the cuts on the ends of each molded edge of the remaining rails *(left)*.

Molding profile

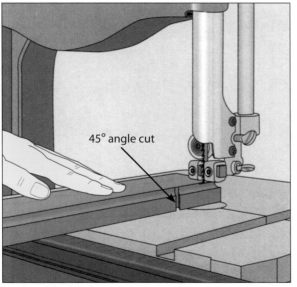

45° angle cut

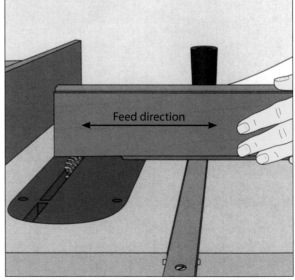

Feed direction

3 Notching the stiles. Leave the table saw blade angled at 45°, measure the width of each rail, and mark a line on the molded edge of its mating stile a corresponding distance from the end. Cut into the molded edge at the line, making certain that the cut will not mar the face of the stile. Slice off most of the strip of molding between the 45° cut and each end of the stile with a band saw *(above, left)*. Smooth the cut edge using the table saw. Leaving the rip fence in place, hold the stile flush against the miter gauge, and slide the stock back and forth across the blade *(above, right)*. Repeat the process for all the stiles.

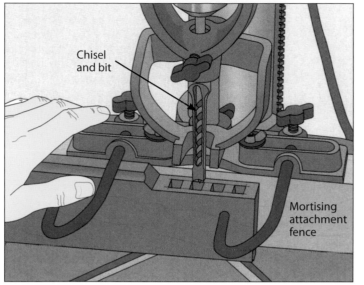

Chisel
and bit

Mortising
attachment
fence

4 Cutting mortises in the stiles. Use one of the tenons you cut in step 1 as a guide to outlining the mortises on the edges of the stiles. To make the job easier, clamp all the stiles together face to face with their ends aligned. Install a mortising attachment on your drill press and clamp one stile to the fence, centering the mortise outline under the chisel and bit. Make the drilling depth $\frac{1}{16}$ inch more than the tenon length; make a cut at each end of the mortise before boring out the waste in between *(left)*. Repeat the procedure to cut the remaining mortises.

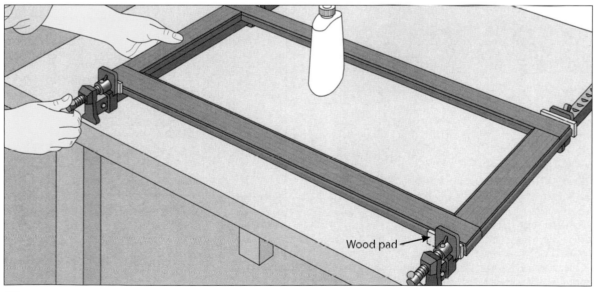

Wood pad

5 Gluing up the doors. Test-assemble the doors and use a chisel to pare away some wood from any overly tight joint. Once you are satisfied with the fit, sand any surfaces that will be difficult to reach when the doors have been glued up, and spread glue on all the contacting surfaces of the joints. Reassemble the doors and set each one on two bar clamps, aligning the bars with the rails. Using wood pads to protect the stock, tighten the clamps *(above)* until a thin glue bead squeezes out of the joints.

Installing the Doors

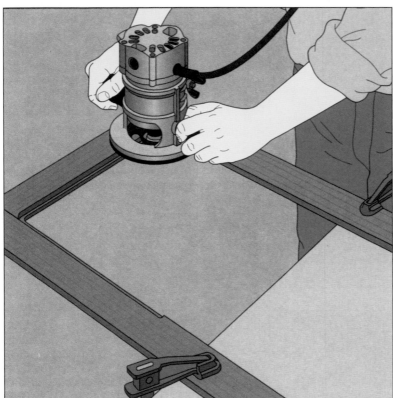

1 Preparing the doors for glass.
Glass panels lie in rabbets and are held in place by thin strips of molding. Clamp one door frame to a work surface, then install a piloted ⅜-inch rabbeting bit in your router and set the depth of cut to the combined thickness of the glass and the molding. Hold the tool firmly with both hands while resting the base plate on the frame near one corner, then guide the bit into the inside edge of the door. Move the router clockwise along the edges *(left)*, keeping the pilot bearing pressed against the stock. Square the corners with a chisel and a wooden mallet. Repeat for the second door.

2 Making the molding. Cut a board longer than you will need for the molding, then install a ½-inch cove bit in your router and mount the tool in a table. Align the bit bearing with the fence and adjust the cutter height to shape the bottom corner of the stock. Mount a featherboard on the table in line with the bit to secure the stock during the cut. Turn on the tool and feed the stock, finishing the pass with a push stick. Shape the other edge of the board the same way *(right)*. Rip the molding from the stock on the table saw and cut the molding to length, mitering the ends at 45°. Cut and fit one piece at a time.

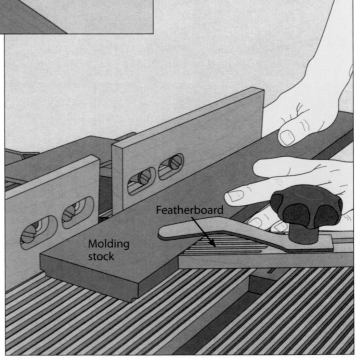

Featherboard

Molding stock

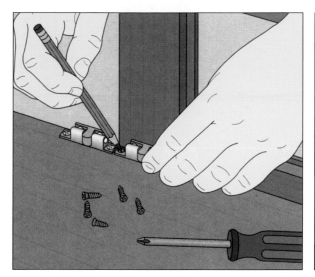

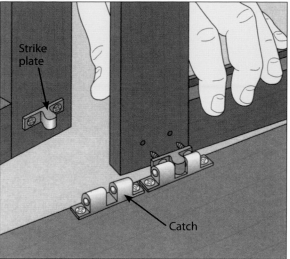

Strike plate

Catch

3 Installing the door catches. Before installing the glass, mount the doors on the bookcase, attaching them with hinges the same way you fastened the fall-front to the desk unit *(page 100)*. It is easier to install the door catches without the glass in place. The ball catches shown above feature a catch fastened to the bottom panel of the bookcase and a strike plate screwed to the inside face of the door stiles; two spring-loaded balls in the catch capture the strike plate when the door is closed. Assemble the catches, hold

one in position against its door stile, then move it toward the back panel by 1/32 inch and mark the screw holes. Drill a pilot hole at each mark and screw the catch in place. Repeat the marking *(above, left)* and fastening process for the other catch. To install the strike plate, insert its screws, engage it with the catch, and close the door; the tips of the screws will mark impressions in the door stile. Drill a pilot hole at each mark and fasten the strike plate to the door. Repeat for the other plate *(above, right)*.

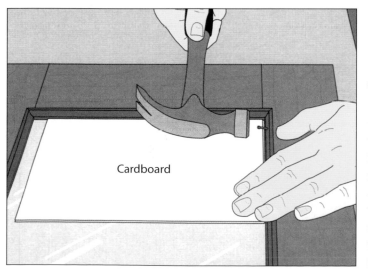

Cardboard

4 Securing the glass. Unscrew the doors from the bookcase and set one door inside-face up on a work surface. Set a drop of clear glazing compound every few inches along the rabbet in the door frame to prevent the glass from rattling. Set the glass and the molding in place and, starting 2 inches from the corners, drill pilot holes at 6-inch intervals through the molding and into the frame. Tack down the molding with brads, using a piece of cardboard to protect the glass from the hammer *(left)*. To finish off the secretary, reinstall the doors.

Anatomy of a Philadelphia-style Highboy

Upper Chest

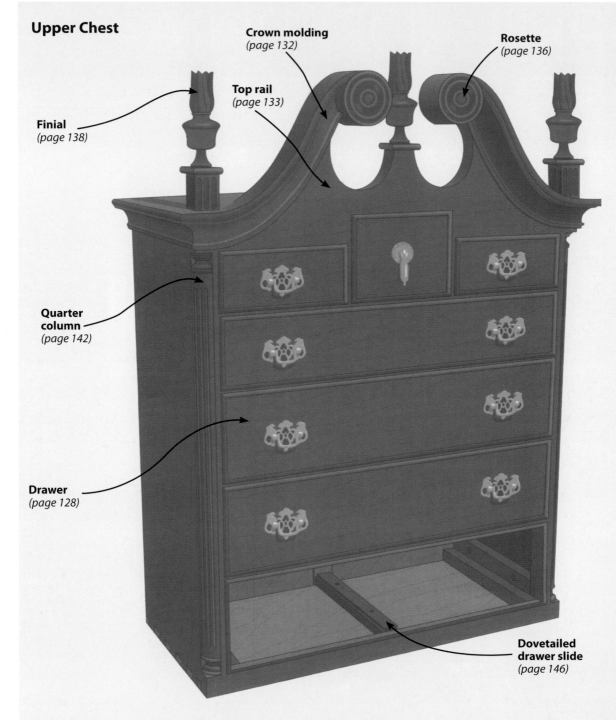

Crown molding
(page 132)

Rosette
(page 136)

Finial
(page 138)

Top rail
(page 133)

Quarter column
(page 142)

Drawer
(page 128)

Dovetailed drawer slide
(page 146)

Lower Chest

Cockbeading
(page 126)

Quarter column
(page 142)

Applied molding
(page 146)

Shell carving
(page 145)

Bottom rail
(page 124)

Knee block
(page 125)

Cabriole leg
(page 120)

Assembling the Upper Chest

The highboy's upper chest has two major components: a large carcase and an elaborate face frame that fits within it. As shown below, the carcase consists of a top and bottom, two side panels, and two back panels separated by a stile—or muntin. The carcase corners are joined with through dovetail joints, and the back panels sit in rabbets cut around the inside edges of the carcase and muntin. The muntin is attached to the top and bottom of the carcase with mortise-and-tenon joints.

The face frame, shown face-up here and face-down opposite, is built from a top rail, two L-shaped front posts, and a drawer frame for each tier of drawers. The top rail is shaped to accept the crown molding *(page 132)* and rosettes *(page 136)*, both of which are added later. The back face of the top rail is grooved to accept the carcase top, and has a tenon cut in each end to fit in mortises in the two front posts. The L shape of the front posts creates the space for the quarter columns *(page 142)*. The front posts sit in notches cut in the carcase top and bottom.

The drawer's supporting frames are assembled from rails and stiles joined with mortise-and-tenons. Each

frame has an added dovetailed slide *(page 130)*. To anchor the frames to the carcase, two braces are screwed to the top of each one and to the side panels. The drawer frames are notched at the front to accommodate the front posts and screwed to them. The uppermost drawer frame supports three small drawers; it features two dividers and three drawer slides. Once the face frame has been built, it is simply slipped into the carcase (see below) and then screwed to the side of the carcase through the braces.

Construction Detail (Face-up View)

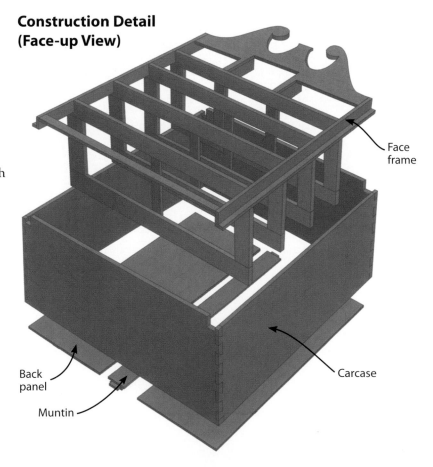

Face frame

Carcase

Back panel

Muntin

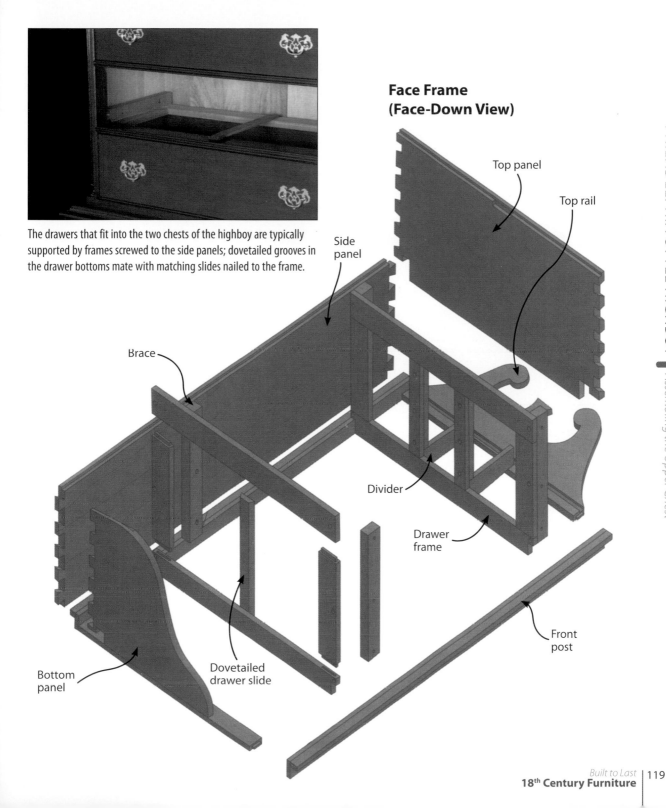

The drawers that fit into the two chests of the highboy are typically supported by frames screwed to the side panels; dovetailed grooves in the drawer bottoms mate with matching slides nailed to the frame.

Face Frame
(Face-Down View)

Top panel

Top rail

Side panel

Brace

Divider

Drawer frame

Front post

Bottom panel

Dovetailed drawer slide

Cabriole Legs

Sawing out the Legs

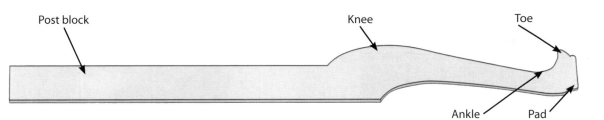

Post block   Knee   Toe

Ankle   Pad

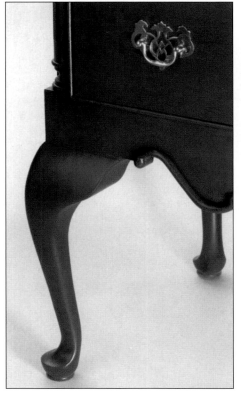

A distinctive feature of Queen Anne style, the tapering, curved cabriole leg has long been considered a challenge for cabinetmakers. But its graceful lines can be cut easily on the band saw and smoothed with hand tools.

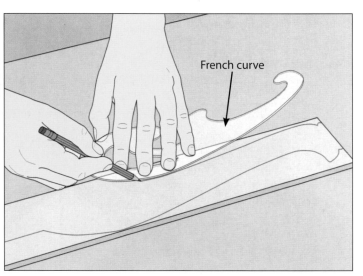

French curve

1 Designing the leg. Make a template from a piece of ¼-inch plywood or hardboard cut to the same length and width as your leg blanks. The design shown above at top will yield an attractive, stable, and well-proportioned leg, but you can alter the pattern to suit your project or copy the design of an existing leg that appeals to you. Begin drawing the leg by outlining the post block. Make its length equal to the width of the lower rail that will be attached to it, plus the height of the lower chest's side panels. The width of the post block should be adequate to accept the rail tenon. Later, it will be notched *(page 124)* to accept the quarter columns of the lower chest. Next, sketch the pad and the toe, then the front of the leg from the toe to the ankle using a french curve; at its narrowest point, the diameter of the ankle should be about two-fifths the stock width. Move on to the knee, sketching a gentle curve from the post block to the front edge of the template about 2 to 3 inches below the block. Then join the knee to the ankle with a relatively straight line. Complete the outline at the back of the leg, from the ankle to the bottom of the post block *(above)*. Experiment until you have a satisfactory design.

2 **Transferring the design to the leg blanks.** Cut out your template on a band saw, then sand the edges to the marked outline. Hold the template flat on one of the inside faces of the leg blank, making sure that the ends of the template and the blank are aligned and that the back of the post block is flush with the inside edge of the blank. Trace along the edges of the template to outline the leg. Turn the blank over and repeat the procedure on the other inside face *(right)*. At this point, some woodworkers prefer to prepare the legs and rails for the joinery before cutting the leg. (It is easier to clamp and cut a mortise in a rectangular leg blank, for example, than to carry out the same procedures on a leg with pronounced curves.) Other woodworkers cut the leg first and then do the joinery.

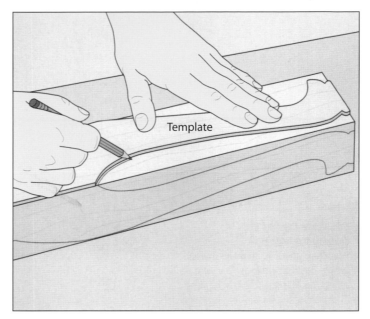

Template

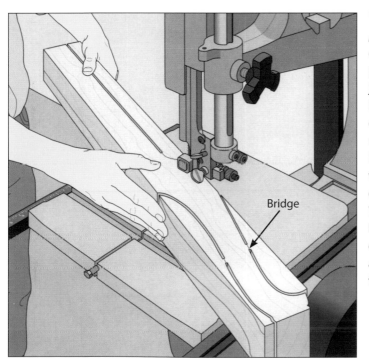

Bridge

3 **Cutting one face.** Set the leg blank on the band saw table with one of the marked outlines facing up and the bottom of the leg pointing away from you. Aligning the saw blade just to the waste side of the marked line for the back of the leg, feed the stock into the blade. Turn off the saw about halfway through the cut and remove the workpiece. Then cut along the same line from the opposite end. To avoid detaching the waste piece from the blank and losing the marked outline on the adjacent face, stop the cut about ½ inch from the first kerf, leaving a short bridge between the two cuts. Retract the workpiece, then cut along the line for the front of the leg *(left)*, again leaving bridges to prevent the waste wood from falling away.

4 **Completing the cuts and severing the bridges.** Turn over the blank so that the marked outline on its adjacent side is facing up. Cut along the marked lines, beginning with those along the front of the leg, then the back *(above)*. This time, complete the cuts, letting the waste fall away. Then rotate the blank and cut through the bridges left during your first cuts *(right)*.

Shaping the Legs

1 **Forming the pad.** Use a compass to outline the circular pad on the bottom of the leg. Then secure the leg in a vise, with the bottom end facing up, and use a backsaw to cut away the bulk of the waste surrounding the outline. Make two series of cuts, starting with four cuts straight into the end of the leg at the corners, then sawing around the end of the leg to sever the corners. Next, secure the leg in a bar clamp, lock the clamp in a vise, and use a patternmaker's rasp to round the corners of the pad. Continue until the pad is circular *(right)*, rotating the leg in the clamp as necessary. Use a file to smooth the pad.

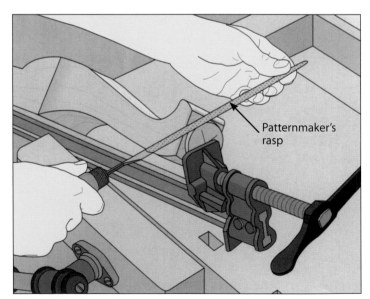

Patternmaker's rasp

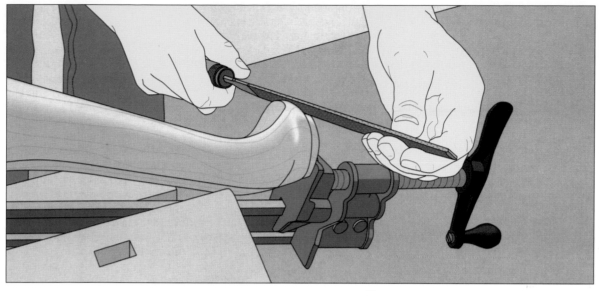

2 Shaping the foot. Reposition the clamp in the vise so the foot is tilted down. Holding the patternmaker's rasp at an angle of approximately 45° to the leg, begin by shaping the contour from the bottom up *(above)*. Rotate the leg in the clamp as necessary so that you can shape the foot all the way around. Smooth the surface using a double-cut flat bastard file, then finish the job with sandpaper, using progressively finer-grit papers.

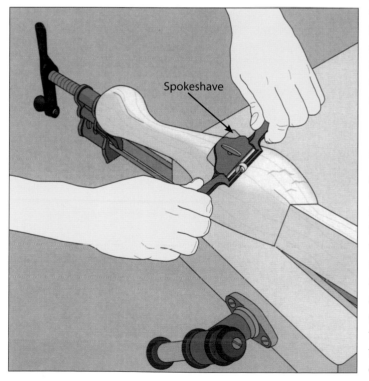

Spokeshave

3 Shaping and smoothing the knee. To finish shaping the cabriole leg and to remove any blemishes left by the band saw blade, smooth the surface of the knee with a spokeshave, following with a rasp and sandpaper. Holding the spokeshave with both hands at the bottom of a curved edge of the leg, push the tool slowly away from you, cutting a thin shaving *(left)*. Make a series of overlapping passes, working with the grain until the surface is smooth. Turn the leg in the bar clamp to clean up the other edges. Use the rasp to smooth an area that the spokeshave cannot reach. Complete the job with sandpaper.

Assembling the Lower Chest

Once the cabriole legs are completed and the cavities for the quarter columns are routed in the post blocks, the lower chest can be glued up. The bottom drawer frame contains dust panels and is divided into sections for three drawers. Like the drawer frames of the upper chest, the top frame features a dovetailed drawer slide. The frames are screwed to braces that are attached to the side panels. The legs are grooved to accept the entire thickness of the back panels and rabbets in the side panels. The legs also feature mortises that mate with tenons cut in the bottom rails. Once the lower chest is glued up, knee blocks are fashioned and attached to the legs *(page 125)*. Cockbeading around the drawers and the shell carving and applied molding on the bottom rail are added later.

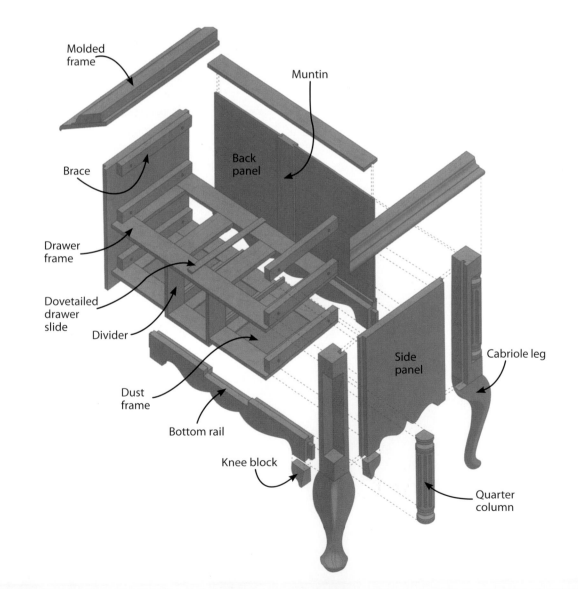

Molded frame

Muntin

Brace

Back panel

Drawer frame

Dovetailed drawer slide

Divider

Dust frame

Side panel

Cabriole leg

Bottom rail

Knee block

Quarter column

Making and Mounting Knee Blocks

1 Designing the knee blocks. The knee blocks, which join the curves of the legs and bottom rails, are designed and cut much like the legs themselves. For a template, place a piece of stiff cardboard in the corner between the leg and adjoining rail and draw a contour line that connects the two pieces. The same template can be used for all the knee blocks. Transfer the line to a wood blank that is as thick as the leg, slightly wider and larger than the area it must fill. Place the blank against the rail and leg so its outside face is flush with the outer part of the leg and draw a second line on the blank using the leg as a guide *(right)*. The grain of the block should be parallel to that of the leg. Saw out the block on the band saw as you did the legs *(page 121)*.

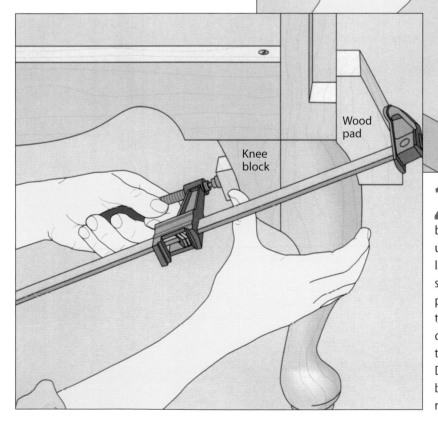

Knee-block blank

Bottom rail

Contour lines

Wood pad

Knee block

2 Mounting the knee blocks. Once all the knee blocks have been cut and smoothed, glue them up one at a time. Apply a thin layer of adhesive to the contacting surfaces, then hold the pieces in place with a clamp. Use wood pads to protect the stock and direct clamping pressure by shaping them to fit flush against the legs *(left)*. Drive a screw through the knee block and into the leg for added reinforcement.

PHILADELPHIA-STYLE HIGHBOY | *Assembling the Lower Chest*

Cockbeading

Cockbeading is a rounded molding that extends beyond the front of the highboy and frames the drawer openings. It is set into rabbets cut along the inside edges of the openings. In addition to providing decoration, cockbeading protects the edges of veneered drawer fronts.

Making and Installing Cockbeading

1 Preparing the drawer openings. Use a router fitted with a ¼-inch piloted rabbeting bit to cut the rabbets around the drawer openings. Set the depth of cut at ½ inch, then attach a square piece of ¼-inch clear acrylic to the tool's base plate *(inset)*. Make this auxiliary sub-base large enough to keep the tool flat and stable during the operation. Set the chest on its back on a work surface. Starting at the corner of one drawer opening, rest the router on the chest with the bit just clear of the workpiece. Grip the tool firmly with both hands and turn it on, guiding the bit into the wood. Once the pilot bearing butts against the stock, feed the router toward the adjacent corner, keeping the sub-base flat *(right)*. Continue around the opening until you reach your starting point. Cut rabbets around the other drawer openings the same way, then square the corners with a chisel.

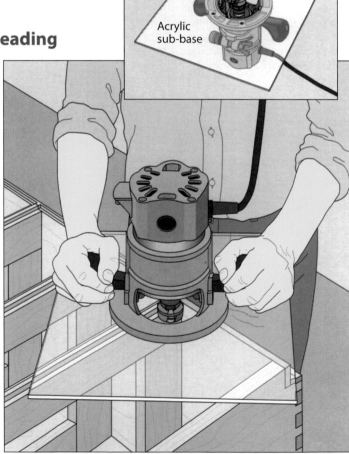

Acrylic sub-base

2 **Making the cockbeading.** Make enough cockbeading from ¼-inch-thick stock to fit in all the rabbets cut in step 1. The cockbeading is best shaped using molding cutters on the table saw. (Do not use narrow stock; instead, cut pieces that are at least 4 inches wide and then rip the cockbeading from them.) Install an auxiliary wood fence and fit the molding head with cutters on your table saw. Raise the head into the wood fence to notch it. Use a featherboard to secure the workpiece; screw it to a shim so that pressure will be applied against the middle of the workpiece. Make a few test passes with scrap stock to set the width of cut. For the first pass, center the board edge over a cutter, then butt the fence against the face of the stock. Hold the board flush against the fence and the table as you feed it into the cutters *(right)*. Experiment with different cutting widths until the edge of the stock is properly rounded, then shape both edges of each workpiece. Once all your stock has been milled, install a rip blade on the saw and cut the cockbeading from the boards, making it wide enough to protrude by ¼ inch from the drawer openings when glued into the rabbets.

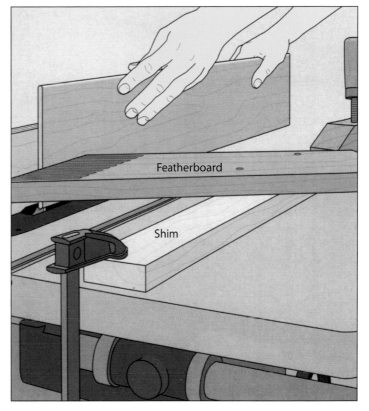

Featherboard

Shim

Spring clamp

3 **Mounting the cockbeading.** Cut the cockbeading to length, mitering the ends with the table saw or a backsaw and miter box. It is easiest to cut and fit one piece at a time, making sure you align the mitered ends with the corners of the rabbets. Spread a little glue on the contacting surfaces and insert one strip at a time, securing the pieces in place with spring clamps at 6-inch intervals *(left)*.

PHILADELPHIA-STYLE HIGHBOY | *Cockbeading*

Drawers

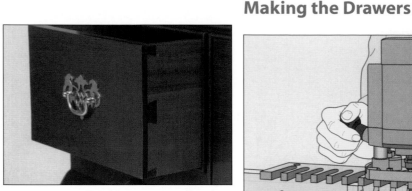

The highboy's drawers exemplify classic cabinetmaking techniques. The corners are joined with through dovetails and the end grain of the tail boards is then hidden with a false front. A dovetailed runner attached to the bottom glides along a mating slide fastened to the frame.

Making the Drawers

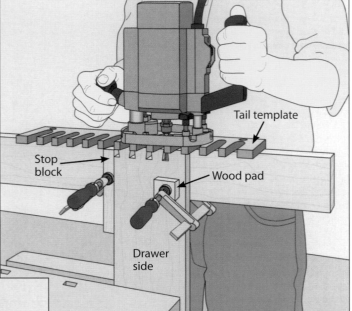

Tail template

Stop block

Wood pad

Drawer side

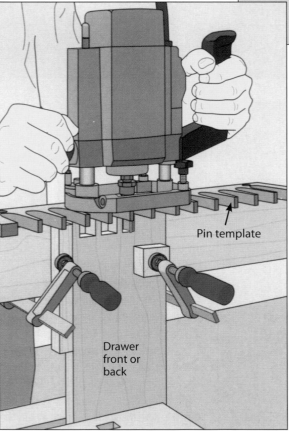

Pin template

Drawer front or back

1 Cutting the dovetail joints. Size the drawer parts to fit the openings in the chests, then rout the dovetails, cutting the pins in the front and back pieces and the tails in the sides. A set of commercial templates like the one shown on this page makes the job simple and ensures accurate results. Attach the pin and tail templates to backup boards following the manufacturer's instructions. Secure one of the drawer sides end-up in a vise. Clamp the backup board to the stock, making sure there are half-tails at either end; the template and backup board should be flush against the workpiece. Protecting the stock with a wood pad, butt a stop block against the drawer side and clamp it to the support board to help you align subsequent cuts. Install the dovetail bit and template guide supplied with the jig and cut the tails, feeding the tool in and out of the template slots *(above)*. Cut the remaining tails the same way. Then use one of the completed tail boards to outline the pins on one drawer front or back. Secure the pin board in the vise and clamp the pin template to the stock, aligning the jig fingers with the marked outline. Install the straight bit supplied with the jig and rout out the waste between the pins *(left)*. Repeat at the other end and for the remaining fronts and backs.

2 Preparing the drawers for bottom panels.

Dry-fit the parts of each drawer and clamp the unit, aligning the bars of the clamps with the front and back pieces; remember to protect the stock with wood pads. Then rout a groove for the bottom panel along the inside of the drawer. Fit a router with a three-wing slotting cutter and mount the tool in a table. Adjust the cutting height to leave the thickness of the drawer runners you will make in step 3 below the groove. Set the drawer right-side up on the table and, starting at the middle of one drawer side, feed the stock into the cutter. Keeping the pilot bearing butted against the workpiece, feed the drawer clockwise *(right)*. Continue pivoting the drawer on the table until you return to your starting point.

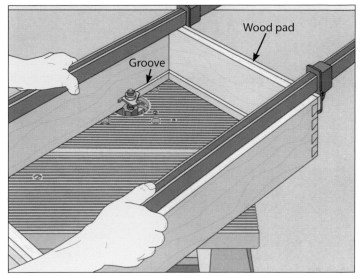

3 Making the drawer runners and slides.

Mounting the drawers in the highboy requires two additional components for each drawer: a runner with a dovetailed groove on the drawer bottom and a matching slide for the frame. Prepare the runner first; it should be as long as the drawer sides and the same thickness as the gap between the bottom panel and the bottom edge of the drawer. To cut the groove in the runner, install a dovetail bit in a router and mount the tool in a table. Set the cutting depth at one-half the runner's thickness. Adjust the fence to center the groove in the runner and make two passes to rout it, using a push block to feed the stock *(left)*. Make the matching slide on the table saw, using stock one-half as thick as the runner. Adjust the blade to the same angle as the sides of the groove, then make two passes to cut the slide, positioning the rip fence on the left-hand side of the blade so the cutting edge is angled away from the fence. Feed the stock using a push stick *(inset)*.

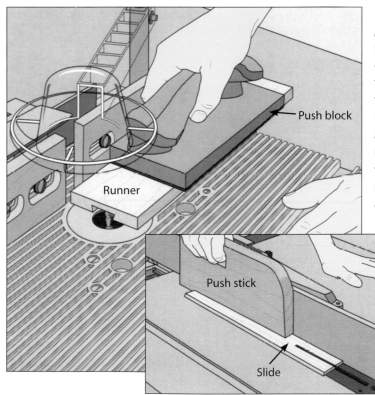

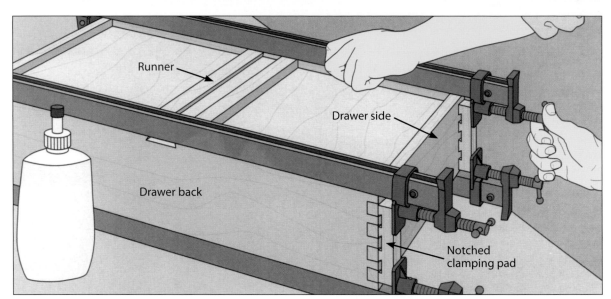

Runner

Drawer side

Drawer back

Notched clamping pad

4 Gluing up the drawers. For the bottom panel of each drawer, cut a piece of ¼-inch plywood to fit the opening, adding the depth of the grooves to its length and width. Dry-fit and clamp the drawer again, position the runner across the bottom panel, and mark the sides of the runner's dovetailed groove on the drawer back. Disassemble the drawer and use a chisel to extend the dovetailed groove through the drawer back. If you wish to install drawer stops *(page 131)*, prepare them now. Then glue up the drawer as you did the chests, adding some adhesive to attach the runners to the drawer bottoms. Notched clamping pads will ensure that pressure is only applied to the tail boards *(above)*.

5 Installing the drawer slides. Once the adhesive has dried, slip each drawer slide into its runner on the drawer bottom and install the drawer in the highboy. Mark the location of the slide on the front and back of the drawer frame, then remove the drawer. Remove the slide and center it on the frame between the alignment marks. Apply a thin layer of glue on the contacting surfaces and secure the slide in place with clamps *(right)*. Once the clamps have been tightened, screw the slide to the front and back of the frame.

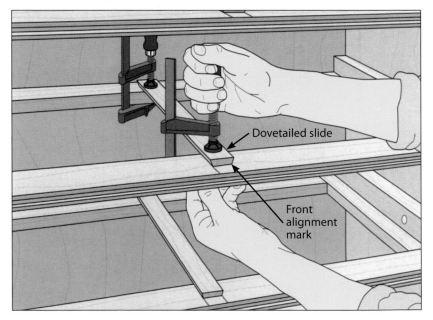

Dovetailed slide

Front alignment mark

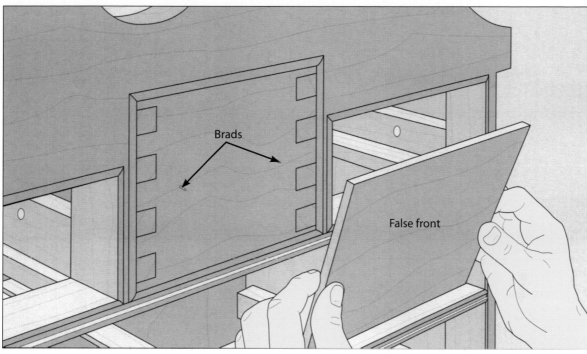

Brads

False front

Shop Tip

Adjustable drawer stop

To keep a drawer from being pulled right out, attach a simple stop to the frame. Before gluing up the drawer, cut a 1-inch-square notch in the middle of the top edge of the drawer back. Saw the stop from scrap, making it longer and narrower than 1 inch. Mount the stop to the bottom of the frame or panel under which the drawer will slide. Line it up with the notch in the drawer back. Screw the stop in place, leaving the fastener loose enough so the stop can be rotated. When you install the drawer, turn the stop so that the long edge is parallel to the drawer sides. Once the stop passes through the notch, turn it 90° so its long edge is parallel to the back.

6 **Installing the false fronts.** Attach a false front to each drawer to conceal the end grain of the drawer sides. Set the drawer face up on a work surface and drive two brads into the drawer front, leaving their heads protruding. Make sure the brads are not located where the drawer pull will be installed, then snip off the heads and reinstall the drawer. Cut the false front to the right size, then carefully position it over the drawer front *(above)*. Once you are satisfied with the placement, press firmly; the pointed ends of the brads will punch impressions into the back of the false front. Remove the drawer and glue the false front in place, aligning the impressions with the brads.

Crown Molding

The crown molding—or pediment—on each side of the highboy front is actually built up from four separate pieces of wood. The broken swan-neck face molding that curves upwards from the front corner to the rosette is made from two pieces of molding glued together. With the help of a template cut on the band saw, the molding pieces are shaped on a pin router *(page 133)*. The moldings on both sides of the highboy, called the returns, also consist of two pieces glued together. They are installed with dovetailed slides that fit into matching grooves in the upper chest *(page 135)*.

A Collection of Crown Molding Styles

Triangular pediment

Latticed broken pediment

Broken pediment

Scrolled broken pediment

Face Moldings

1 **Shaping the first piece of molding.** For a template, trace the contours of the upper rail onto a piece of ¾-inch plywood. Add a cutting line to represent the bottom edge of the first piece of molding *(inset)*, then saw the template in two along the line and discard the bottom half. Outline the template on the stock you will use for the molding and cut it to size. Next, screw the molding blank atop the template, making sure the fasteners will be clear of the router bit. Install a piloted panel-raising bit and mount the router in a pin routing attachment. Follow the manufacturer's directions for setting the depth of cut, then place the starter pin in the table on the infeed side of the bit. As you feed the molding blank into the bit, brace the template against the pin *(right)*, keeping the molding blank against the bit's pilot bearing. Make light cuts, using as many passes as necessary to reach your final depth. Repeat the process with the template reversed to shape the molding for the other side of the chest front. Then shape the side moldings using the same setup and a straight template of the same thickness.

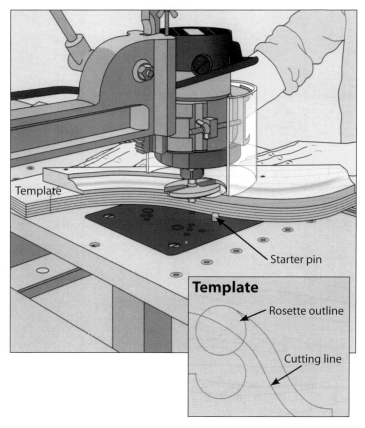

Template

Starter pin

Template

Rosette outline

Cutting line

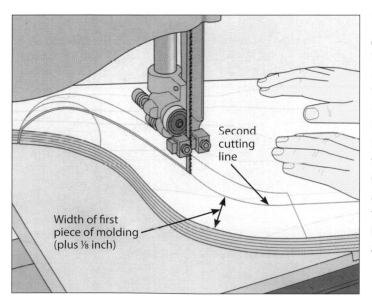

Second cutting line

Width of first piece of molding (plus ⅛ inch)

2 **Shaping the second piece of molding.** The piece of molding that is glued to the first one to build up the face molding is shaped by the same process used in step 1. Unscrew the first piece from the template, then draw a cutting line for the second piece, offsetting the line by the width of the first piece plus ⅛ inch. Band saw along the mark *(left)*. Cut and shape the second piece of molding as you did the first: Cut it to width, attach the piece to the template, and shape it on the pin routing attachment—this time, using a round-over bit. Once the molding has been shaped, unscrew it from the template and saw it to final width.

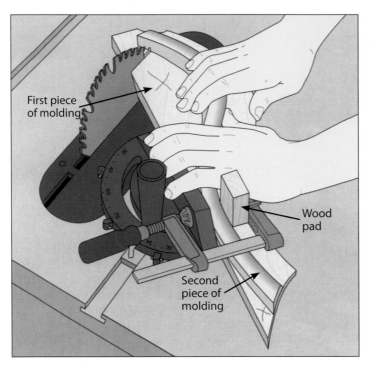

First piece of molding

Wood pad

Second piece of molding

3 Preparing the face moldings for installation. Glue the parts of the face molding together and hold them securely with clamps. Once the adhesive has cured, each piece of face molding must be cut at one end to meet the side molding and at the other end to fit around the rosette. For the side molding-end, set up your table saw for a compound cut by angling the blade to 45° and the miter gauge to the angle formed between the straight edge of the molding and the side of the carcase when the molding is held in place. Clamp the face molding to the miter gauge, protecting the stock with a wood pad. Since the top of the molding is straight and the bottom is curved, you will have to feed the stock with what would normally be the trailing end first. Hold the gauge and molding securely, and push the stock into the cut, keeping your hands well clear of the blade *(left)*. Then band saw the waste (marked with Xs).

Installing the Crown Molding

1 Installing the face molding. Once all the moldings have been shaped and cut to length, install the quarter columns *(page 142)*. Then clamp the side molding in place using protective wood pads. Next, mount the face molding to the rail as you did the false fronts of the drawers *(page 131)*, using brads to align the stock *(right)*. The mitered end of the face molding should rest flush against the end of the side molding. Glue and clamp the face molding to the rail.

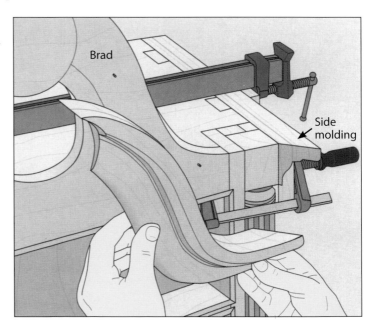

Brad

Side molding

2 **Preparing the upper chest for the side molding.** The side molding is attached to the chest with a sliding dovetail joint to allow the carcase to expand and contract because of changes in humidity without breaking the mitered joints on the front corners. The dovetailed groove is cut in the chest side with a router. Install a dovetail bit, then attach a commercial edge guide to the tool's base plate and screw a wood extension to the guide fence to increase its bearing surface. Set the chest on its side and place the router on top. Adjust the edge guide so that the groove will be cut just below the corner joint. With the bit clear of the chest, start at the back and feed the cutting edges into the side panel, pulling the edge guide extension flush against the top panel. Continue toward the front of the chest *(right)*, stopping the cut a little past the halfway point.

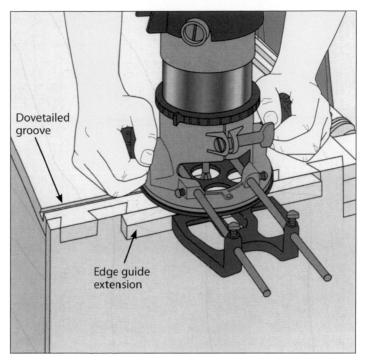

Dovetailed groove

Edge guide extension

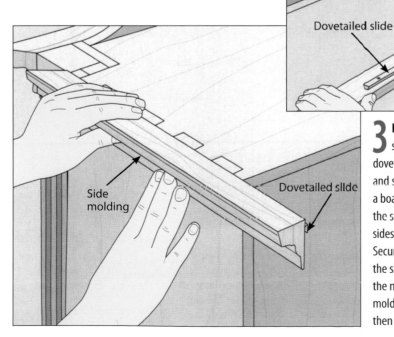

Dovetailed slide

Side molding

Dovetailed slide

3 **Installing the side molding.** To produce a slide to match the groove in the chest, leave the dovetail bit in the router, mount the tool in a table, and shape the slide in two passes along the edge of a board. Then rip the slide from the board. Position the side molding against the chest and mark the sides of the groove on the back of the molding. Secure the molding face-down in a vise and screw the slide to the back *(inset)*, aligning it between the marks. Spread glue on the mitered end of the molding and on the first 2 inches of its back face, then slide it in place *(left)* and clamp securely.

PHILADELPHIA-STYLE HIGHBOY | *Crown Molding*

Rosettes

Rosettes are an ornamental feature common to many furniture styles. They can take many shapes and be produced in various ways. The concentric circles of the rosette at left were turned on a lathe, creating a pattern that flows seamlessly from the graceful curves of the crown molding.

Making the Rosettes

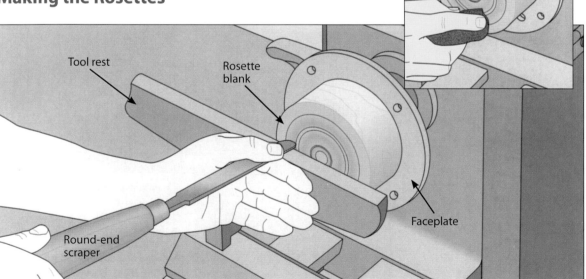

Turning the rosettes. Cut the rosette blanks to fit on the end of the face moldings. Attach a blank to the center of a lathe faceplate, then mount the plate on the machine. Adjust the tool rest so the top face of the scraper you will use is level with the center of the blank. The rest should be as close to the wood as possible without touching it. Switch on the lathe. Holding the tip of a round-end scraper against the blank, round over the rosette's outside edge, and then cut the concentric rings on its face *(above)*. Hold the scraper blade on the tool rest to keep it steady. Cut on the left-hand side of the blank to prevent the scraper from kicking up. Once the rings have been carved, remove the tool rest and smooth the face of the blank with fine-grit sandpaper *(inset)*.

Mounting the Rosettes

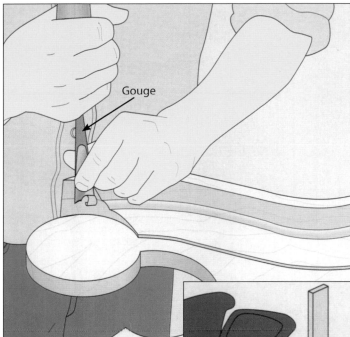

Gouge

1 **Preparing the face moldings for the rosettes.** Once both rosettes have been turned, use a gouge to shape the rounded end of the moldings so that the contacting surfaces fit snugly together. Set the upper chest face-up on a work surface and hold the gouge upright as you pare away wood from the molding *(left)* until it fits flush against the rosette.

2 **Gluing up the rosettes.** Position each rosette in turn on the chest so that its wood grain runs in the same direction as the face molding. This will create the impression that the two parts are one continuous piece. Mark the rosette where it touches the molding, then apply some glue to the contacting surfaces of both pieces. Use one clamp to secure the rosette in place and a second *(right)* to keep it from sliding forward or backward. Protect the stock with wood pads.

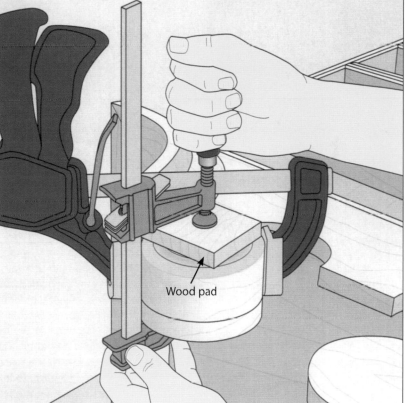

Wood pad

Finials

Traditionally used to decorate the corners of furniture, finials take a variety of forms, including flame-and-urn, acorn, pineapple, and plume. The finial above incorporates two shapes, a flame-and-urn on a fluted pommel base. This example is produced from the bottom up: First, the flutes of the pommel are grooved on a router table *(right)*, and then the flame and urn are turned on a lathe *(page 139)*. Finally, the finished shape of the flame is carved by hand *(page 141)*.

Shaping the Pommel

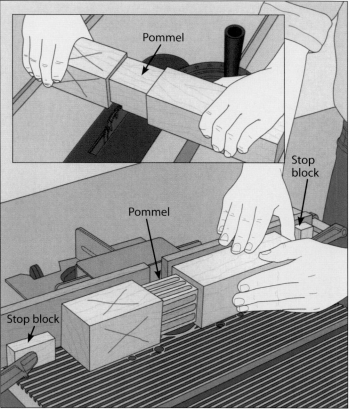

Cutting the flutes. Make a blank for each finial that is slightly larger than the finished dimensions. Mark the top and bottom of the pommel on the blank and use Xs to indicate the waste section below the pommel. Use the dado head in a table saw to reduce the blank's thickness between the two marks. Set the cutting depth at $3/8$ inch. Feed the blank with the miter gauge, cutting away the waste with overlapping passes on each face *(inset)*. The flutes are cut with a core box bit in a table-mounted router. Set the cutting depth at $1/4$ inch. Align the pommel over the bit for the first set of outside flutes and lock the fence against the blank. To ensure that all the flutes will be the same length, clamp a stop block to the fence at each end of the blank. Turn on the router and lower the blank onto the bit with its trailing end against the stop block closest to you and its edge against the fence. Feed the blank until it contacts the other stop block. Lift the blank, then rotate it and repeat the process until one set of outside flutes is finished. Reposition the fence once to rout the middle flutes and again for the second set of outside flutes *(above)*.

Turning the Flame-and-Urn

1 Turning the cylinder. Cut off most of the waste section below the pommel, leaving a couple of inches for a round tenon. Mount the blank on a lathe and adjust the tool rest as close to the workpiece as possible without touching it. Use a roughing-out gouge to round the corners of the blank above the pommel. Turn on the lathe and hold the tip of the gouge against the rotating blank. Begin with the tip of the gouge tilted up, then gradually raise the handle until the bevel under the tip is rubbing against the stock and the cutting edge is slicing into it. Work from the right-hand end of the blank toward the pommel, leaving a square shoulder above the pommel *(right)*. Keep the tool at the same angle to the workpiece throughout the cut. Continue until the blank is cylindrical and smooth.

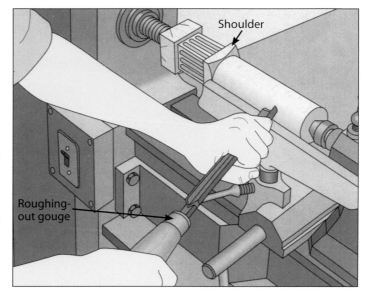

2 Shaping the flame. Leave the blank rotating while you mark the bottom ends of the urn and the flame with a pencil. Use a skew chisel to cut a notch separating the flame and urn, then begin shaping the flame with a spindle gouge *(above)*. The process is the same as for the cylinder in step 1, but instead of holding the tool at a fixed angle to the blank, sweep it from side to side while angling the tip to cut a contour. Continue until the flame has the desired shape.

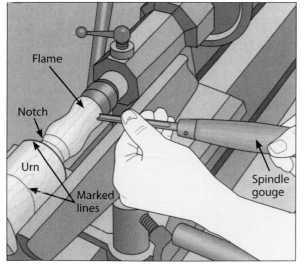

3 Shaping the urn. Shape the urn with a spindle gouge as you did the flame. Then use a skew chisel to cut a notch defining the lower end of the urn. Pressing the chisel firmly against the tool rest, hold the short point of the tip against the blank to cut the V-shaped notch; keep the bevel on the back of the blade rubbing against the stock to help control the cut *(above)*. Then use the skew chisel and spindle gouge to shape beads below the urn.

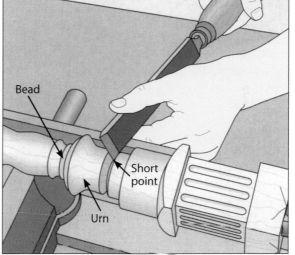

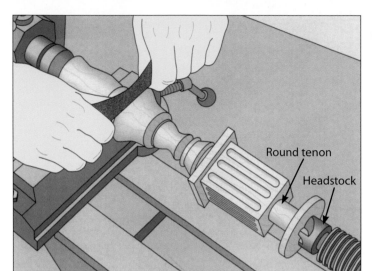

Round tenon

Headstock

4 Turning the tenon and smoothing the finial. Use a parting tool to turn a ¾-inch-long round tenon below the pommel, leaving a thin disk of wood against the headstock of the lathe. Then remove the tool rest and smooth the surface of the finial with sandpaper, using progressively finer grits. Fold the paper to reach around the beads and into crevices *(left)*. To finish smoothing the piece, hold a handful of wood shavings under the rotating finial and allow it to rub against the shavings. Combined with your skin oils, the shavings will impart a smooth finish to the surface. Once the job is done, turn off and unplug the lathe, but leave the blank mounted on the tool.

Carving the Flame

1 Sketching the pattern. To help you carve the flame, mark a grid of ½-inch squares on the entire surface of the flame section. Then draw in four equally spaced spiral lines from the bottom to the top of the section to delineate the hollows you will carve in step 2; the lines should intersect opposite corners of each square *(right)*.

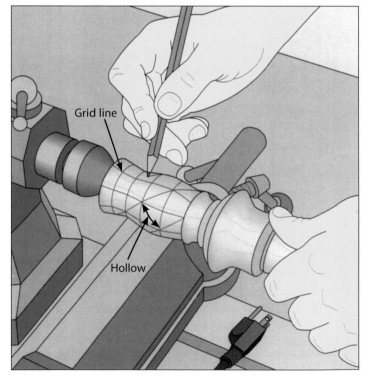

Grid line

Hollow

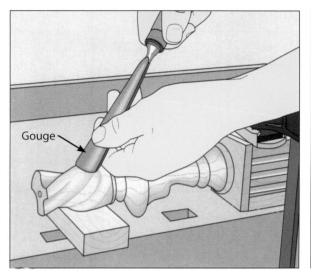

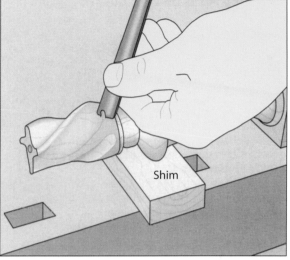

2 Carving the flame. Remove the finial from the lathe and saw off the waste disk below the tenon. Then clamp the finial to a work surface, using shims to hold it parallel to the benchtop. Carve the hollows between the grid lines with two gouges, starting with a wide-blade tool *(above, left)*. Work parallel to the wood grain as much as possible; rotate and re-clamp the finial so that you can reach the entire surface. Use a narrower gouge to carve a sharply defined ridge between each hollow *(above, right)*. Work from the bottom to the top of the flame, bringing each ridge to a point. Then hollow out the top end to remove the hole left by the lathe's tailstock and smooth the flame with sandpaper.

Mounting the Finials

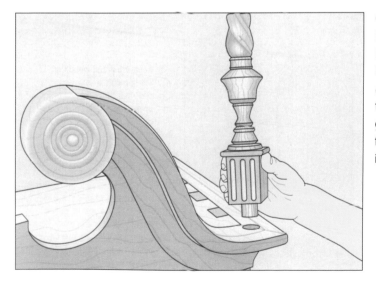

Gluing the finials to the chest. For each finial, bore a hole into the top of the chest with a spade bit the same diameter as the tenon on the finial. Locate the hole directly above the quarter column *(page 142)*. This will create the impression that the column and finial are a single piece. Spread glue on the tenon and the sides of the hole, then fit the finial in place *(left)*. Use a clamp to hold it in position until the adhesive cures.

Quarter Columns

Making and Installing the Quarter Columns

1 Making the columns. Cut a blank several inches longer than the finished length of the columns, and wide and thick enough for the number of quarter columns you need. Rip the blank into quarters, joint the inside surfaces of the pieces, then glue and clamp them back together with newspaper in between *(inset, top)*. This will enable you to pull the columns apart easily. Once the glue is dry, mount the blank on a lathe. Mark two lines on the blank for the length of the column and indicate the waste with Xs *(inset, bottom)*. Drive screws through the waste sections to hold the quarters together. Adjust a set of outside calipers to the desired diameter of the column, then turn the blank into a cylinder as you did for the finials *(page 139)*. Periodically turn off the lathe and use the calipers to check the diameter of the blank *(right)*. Once you have reduced the blank to the correct diameter, turn two beads at each end using a skew chisel and a fingernail gouge. Then cut the flutes in the blank, either by hand using a gouge or with the router and jig shown on page 143.

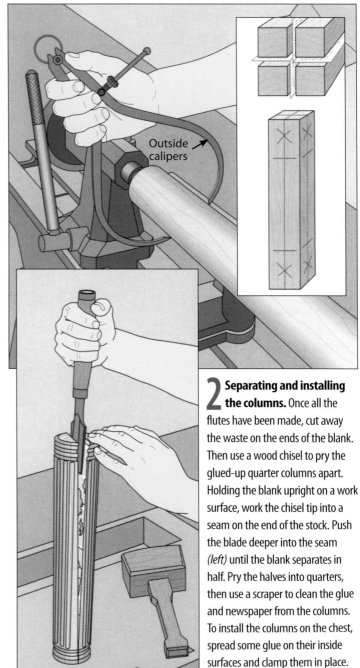

Outside calipers

Fluted quarter columns add a strong visual framework to the highboy.

2 Separating and installing the columns. Once all the flutes have been made, cut away the waste on the ends of the blank. Then use a wood chisel to pry the glued-up quarter columns apart. Holding the blank upright on a work surface, work the chisel tip into a seam on the end of the stock. Push the blade deeper into the seam *(left)* until the blank separates in half. Pry the halves into quarters, then use a scraper to clean the glue and newspaper from the columns. To install the columns on the chest, spread some glue on their inside surfaces and clamp them in place.

A Router-Lathe Jig for Fluting Quarter Columns

With the box-like jig shown below, you can rout flutes in a quarter column blank while it is mounted on the lathe. Cut the parts of the jig from ¾-inch plywood, except for the top, which is made from ¼-inch clear acrylic. The jig should be long and wide enough to support the router and high enough to hold the tool just above the column blank when the jig bottom rests on the lathe bed. Once the top, bottom, and sides are assembled, add two vertical braces to make the jig more rigid. Rest the jig on the lathe bed.

Install a double-bearing piloted fluting bit in your router, drill a bit clearance hole through the jig top, and screw the tool's base plate to the jig. The router should be positioned so the bit will lie alongside the column blank when the jig is used. Next, mark cutting lines for the flutes on the blank, then mount the blank on the lathe. Be sure all tools

are unplugged during setup. Adjust the cutting depth on the router so the bit is aligned with the cutting line at the midpoint of the blank. Tighten a handscrew around the lathe drive shaft to keep it from rotating. Clamp stop blocks to the lathe bed so that all the flutes will be the same length.

To use the jig, butt it against one stop block, turn on the router and push on the side of the jig to feed the bit into the blank. Once the pilots are flush against the stock, slide the jig along the lathe bed until it contacts the other stop block. Keep the pilots pressed against the stock as you rout the flute. Turn off the router, remove the handscrew and rotate the blank by hand to align the next cutting line with the bit, and reinstall the handscrew. Cut the remaining flutes (below).

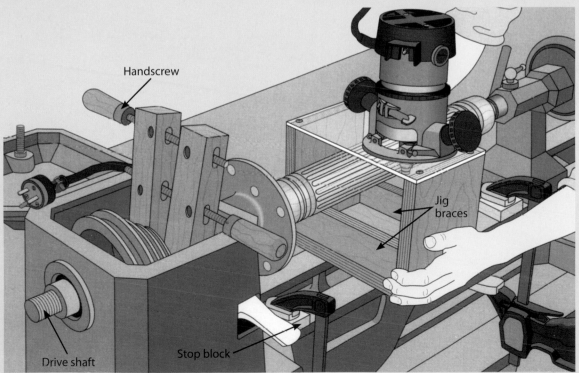

Handscrew

Jig braces

Drive shaft

Stop block

Applied Sculptures

Scallop shells, stylized sunbursts, and fans were popular carvings applied to Queen Anne, Georgian, and Chippendale furniture throughout the 18th Century. Carved by hand, decorative motifs like the one at right were commonly found on the aprons of highboys. They were also used to adorn the knees of cabriole legs and the fronts of central drawers.

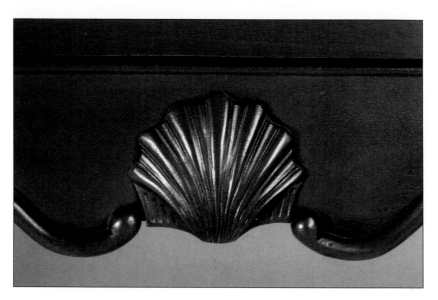

A Sampling of Fan and Shell Motifs

Queen Anne scallop shell

Regency flower

Louis XIV shell

Queen Anne fan

Chippendale scallop shell

Chippendale shell

Making and Applying a Scallop Shell

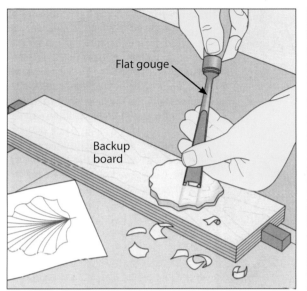

Flat gouge

Backup board

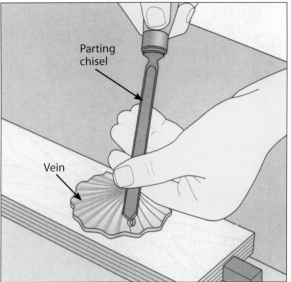

Parting chisel

Vein

1 Sculpting the shell surface. Draw the shell pattern full-size on a sheet of paper, then transfer your design to a hardwood blank of the desired thickness. Cut the edges of the blank on the band saw and fasten it to a backup board. Secure the backup board to a work surface. Start sculpting the surface of the shell using a flat gouge *(above, left)*,

working in the direction of the wood grain. Then transfer the vein lines from your pattern to the blank, and use a parting chisel to etch the lines into the wood *(above, right)*. Cut from the bottom of the blank to the top; to avoid tearout, stop each cut near the top and complete it from the opposite direction.

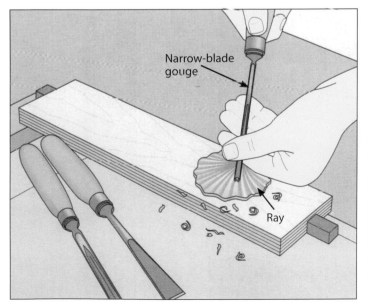

Narrow-blade gouge

Ray

2 Rounding the rays. Once all the veins have been cut, use the flat gouge to round the contours of the rays between the vein lines. Start by making the surfaces of all the rays convex (or crowning outward). To finish carving the pattern, carve a concave valley into every second ray with a narrow-blade gouge *(left)*. The surfaces of adjacent rays should curve in opposite directions, alternating between convex and concave. Use a parting tool to carve the veins in the wings at the lower sides of the shell *(photo, page 144)*. Once you are satisfied with the shape of the shell, sand the surface lightly. Then detach it from the backup board and glue it in place on the front of the lower chest, using brads to help locate it *(page 131)* and clamps to hold it in place while the adhesive dries.

Making and Mounting the Applied Molding

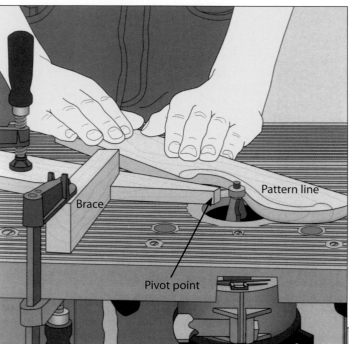

Brace

Pattern line

Pivot point

1 Shaping the volutes on the router table.
The curved moldings, called volutes, which decorate the apron of the lower chest, are shaped partially with the router, as shown at left, and partially by hand, as in step 3. Start by making a cardboard template of the molding, then transfer your pattern to a workpiece of the desired thickness. Leave enough waste on the stock to feed it safely across the router table. Cut along one of the pattern lines on the band saw, exposing one edge of the molding. To shape this edge, install a piloted round-over bit in a router and mount the tool in a table. Rather than making the cut freehand, clamp a pivot point to the table in line with the bit, using a brace to steady it. As you feed the work-piece into the bit, brace the stock against the pivot point *(left)*. Make sure you keep the workpiece flush against the bit pilot.

2 Cutting away the remaining waste. Once you have finished shaping one edge of the volute, detach the molding from the waste using the band saw. To keep the blade from binding in the kerf, make a release cut through the waste, stopping at the pattern line. Then saw along the line, feeding the workpiece with both hands *(right)*. Make sure that neither hand is in line with the blade.

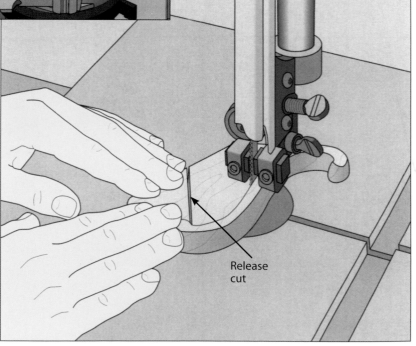

Release
cut

3 **Hand-shaping the second edge.** Secure a backup board to a work surface and clamp the molding to the board. Round over the second edge of the volute with a gouge, copying the profile produced by the router bit in step 1 *(right)*. Shape the edge until its contours are smooth; try as much as possible to cut with the grain. Remove the molding from the backup board and sand the surface lightly.

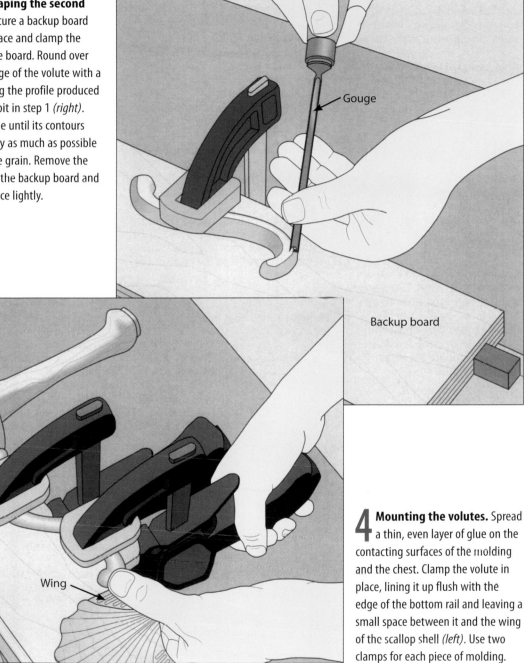

Gouge

Backup board

Wing

4 **Mounting the volutes.** Spread a thin, even layer of glue on the contacting surfaces of the molding and the chest. Clamp the volute in place, lining it up flush with the edge of the bottom rail and leaving a small space between it and the wing of the scallop shell *(left)*. Use two clamps for each piece of molding.

Anatomy of a Pembroke Table

The Pembroke table consists of three main sections: a top, the leg-and-rail assembly, and a drawer. The top is attached to a leaf on each side with a hinged rule joint. The edges of the top are rounded over and the mating edges of the leaves are shaped with a matching cove, forming a seamless joint when the leaves are in the up position. The leaves are supported by fly rails that swing out from the side rails on knuckle joints. As shown opposite, these joints feature interlocking fingers fixed together by a wooden pin.

Each side rail is made up of four individual boards. First, the knuckle joint between the long outer side rail piece and the fly rail is cut and assembled. Then, the short outer side rail piece is sawn to size and the stationary pieces are face-

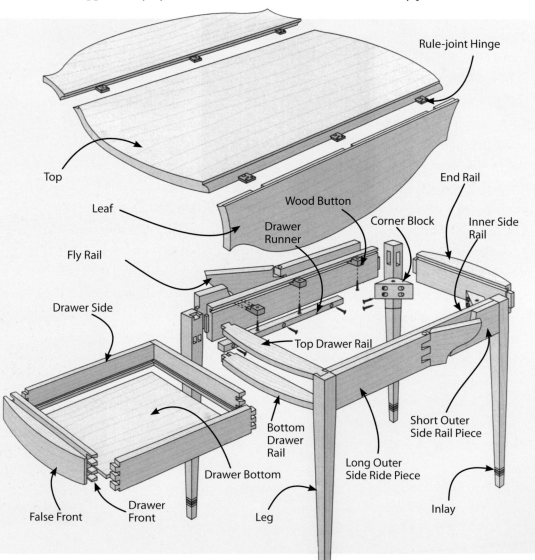

Top

Leaf

Fly Rail

Drawer Side

False Front

Drawer Front

Leg

Bottom Drawer Rail

Drawer Bottom

Wood Button

Drawer Runner

Top Drawer Rail

Corner Block

Rule-joint Hinge

End Rail

Inner Side Rail

Short Outer Side Rail Piece

Long Outer Side Ride Piece

Inlay

glued to the inner side rail. The assembly is then joined to the legs with blind mortise-and-tenons. Wooden corner blocks are screwed to adjoining rails at the back end of the table to keep the corners square.

The top is attached to the rails with wood buttons, which feature a lip that fits into a groove cut along the inside edges of the rails; the buttons

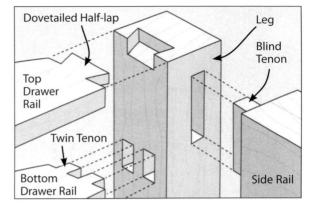

Cutting List

ITEM	QUANTITY	THICKNESS	WIDTH	LENGTH
Corner blocks	2	3"	3"	3"
Drawer: Front and back	2	⅝"	2"	14"
False front	1	1½"	2"	14"
Sides	2	"	2"	18"
Drawer rails*	2	¾"	3"	16"
Runners	2	¾"	1"	21"
Bottom	1	¼"	14"	17¼"
End rail*	1	4⅜"	3"	16"
Fly rails	2	1"	4"	10½"
Inner side rails*	2	1"	4"	32"
Leaves	2	"	10"	41"
Legs	4	1¾"	1¾"	29¼"
Short outer side rail pieces*	2	1"	4"	11¼"
Long outer side rail pieces*	2	1"	4"	16¾"
Top	1	"	20"	41"

*Note: Dimensions include tenon or half-lap lengths.

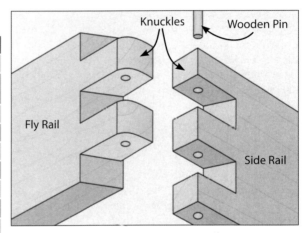

are screwed to the underside of the top. As shown on page 47, pocket holes can also be used.

The dovetailed drawer is supported by wooden runners screwed flush with the bottom edge of the side rails.

The top is attached to the rails with wood buttons, which feature a lip that fits into a groove cut along the inside edges of the rails; the buttons are screwed to the underside of the top. As shown on page 47, pocket holes can also be used.

The dovetailed drawer is supported by wooden runners screwed flush with the bottom edge of the side rails.

Making The Leg-and-Rail Assembly

The legs of a Pembroke table have a delicate look that belies their sturdiness. They are tapered, with a simple banded inlay around each leg about 3 inches from the bottom. The banding includes a ¾-inch-wide dark strip—in this case, walnut— which contrasts with the mahogany. A thin strip of maple frames the walnut. On some Pembroke tables, the inlay was used to mark the transition to a second, steeper taper at the bottom of the leg. Traditionally, legs with a double taper were tapered on the two inside faces above the banding and on all four sides below it. The version shown in this chapter features a single taper on each face.

TAPERING THE LEGS

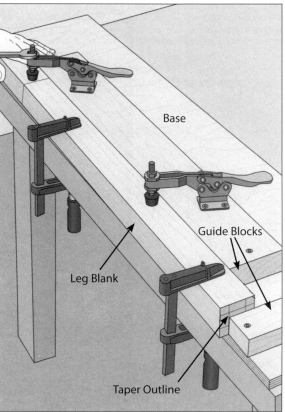

Base

Guide Blocks

Leg Blank

Taper Outline

Once the side rails are assembled, they are joined to the legs with mortise- and-tenons (page 33). So, too, is the end rail, but it must first be bandsawed into a curved shape to complement the curved drawer front at the opposite end of the table (page 36). The drawer rails are fixed to the legs with twin mortise-and-tenons and dovetailed half-laps (page 34).

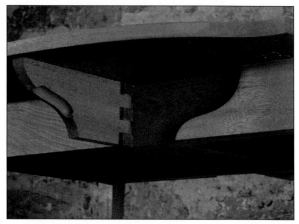

A fly rail holds up one of the leaves of the Pembroke table shown above. The knuckle joint that attaches the fly rail to the side rail is designed to stop pivoting once the fly rail opens to a 90° angle. A recess carved into the curved edge of the fly rail provides a convenient handhold.

1 **Cut your leg blanks to size, referring to the anatomy illustration on page 24.** Mark a line all around each blank 5 inches from the top end to define the square section to which the rails will be joined. Then outline a ¾-inch square on the bottom end of the blank to define the taper. To make the cut on your table saw, use a shop-made jig. Cut the base from ¾-inch plywood, making it longer and wider than the blanks. Set a blank on the base, aligning corresponding taper lines at the top and bottom with the edge of the base. Clamp the blank in place and position the guide blocks against it. Screw the guide blocks to the base, then fasten two toggle clamps to the longer block. Press the toggle clamps down to secure the blank to the jig, tightening the nuts on the clamps with a wrench (above). Remove the bar clamps.

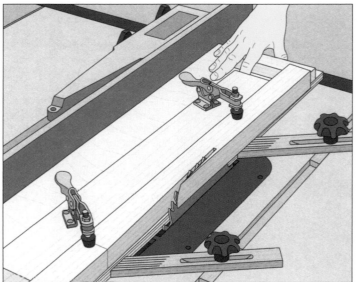

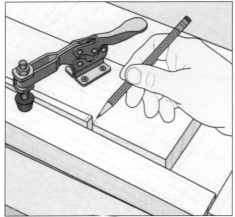

3 Cutting the remaining tapers. Release the toggle clamps, turn the blank to the adjacent side, and reclamp it, this time using a wedge between the long guide block and the tapered part of the blank to compensate for the cut you just made. Mark the location of the broad end of the wedge on the guide block so you can reposition the wedge properly for the remaining two cuts (above). Then taper the second side of the blank. Repeat the process for the remaining sides.

2 Cutting the first taper. Butt the edge of the jig base with the blank against the blade and position the rip fence flush against the opposite edge of the base. To support the blank during the cut, mount two featherboards to the saw table, one on each side of the blade. Taper the first side of the blank by sliding the jig and workpiece across the table, making sure neither hand is in line with the blade (above). **(Caution: Blade guard removed for clarity.)**

Installing Inlay Banding on the Legs

1 Setting up the router table. To cut dadoes in the legs for inlay banding on a router table, install a ¾-inch straight bit in a router and mount the tool in a table. Adjust the cutter for a ⅛-inch-deep cut. Next, attach an extension board to the miter gauge. To ensure that the dadoes are parallel to the ends of the leg, the miter gauge must be set to the appropriate angle. Hold the tapered part of the leg flush against the miter gauge extension while butting the handle of a try square against the leg's square portion. Adjust the miter gauge so the miter bar is parallel to the blade of the square (left).

2 Routing the dadoes.

Position the leg against the miter gauge extension so the bottom end is 3 3/16 inch to the right of the bit. To ensure all the dadoes will be aligned, butt a stop block against the end of the leg and clamp it to the extension. To cut the first dado, hold the leg flush against the extension and stop block, and feed the leg and miter gauge across the table into the bit. Turn the blank to the adjacent side and repeat to rout the remaining dadoes (left).

Stop Block

3 Gluing the banding.

Using a hardwood darker than the leg, cut a rectangular piece of banding for every dado. Saw the banding so the grain will be parallel with the grain of the leg when the pieces are glued in place; they should be the same width as the dadoes, but about 1/4 inch longer and 3/16 inch thick. Spread glue on two pieces of banding, set them in dadoes on opposite sides of the leg and secure them in place with a C clamp (right). Once the adhesive has cured, remove the clamp and trim the ends of the banding flush with the leg by running the adjoining dadoes across the router table again as in step 2. Glue banding into these dadoes, then sand the banding flush with the leg surface.

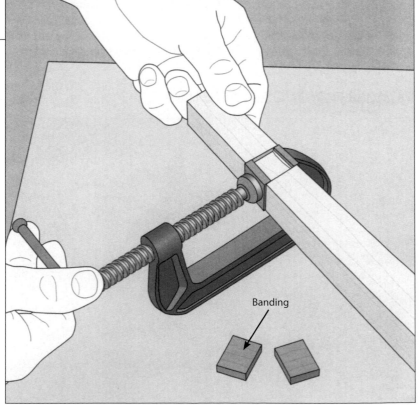

Banding

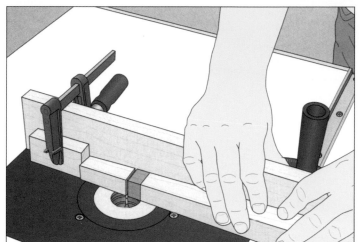

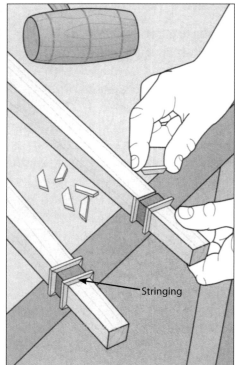

4 Kerfing the legs for the stringing. To accentuate the inlay banding on the legs, install narrow strips of wood called stringing between the banding and the leg. For maximum effect, choose a species that is lighter than the wood you have selected for the table. Using the same procedure you followed in step 2, cut slots for the stringing along the edges of the banding—but this time, with a⅛-inch upcut spiral straight bit in the router. Cut all the slots at the bottom edge of the banding first, then reposition the stop block to rout the remaining slots.

Stringing

5 Installing the stringing. Make the stringing from ⅛-inch- thick, ¼-inch wide wood strips. Using a backsaw in a mini-miter box (like the kind used in dollhouse-building), cut the strips to fit in the slots. Cut and fit one piece at a time, mitering the ends at 45°. Apply glue to the piece, insert it into its slot (above)and tap it into place with a wooden mallet. Once all the stringing is installed and the adhesive has cured, sand the pieces flush with the leg surfaces.

Instead of being cut to fit into a dado in a leg, the commercial inlay veneers shown at left are glued to the sides of a tapered leg blank.

Preparing the Side Rails

Making the Side Rails

1 Marking the knuckle joints.
Butt the mating ends of the fly rail and the long outer side rail piece together, making sure the board edges are aligned. Use reference letters to label the pieces, then mark a shoulder line on each board about 1 inch from their mating ends; use a try square to ensure the lines are perpendicular to the board edges To complete the joint outline, use a tape measure to divide the boards into five equal segments across their width, creating a grid of fingers and notches on the board ends. Mark the waste sections—or notches—with Xs (right)so the fly rail will have three notches and the mating piece two notches.

Long Outer Side Rail Piece

Shoulder Line

Fly Rail

Knuckle Joint Outline

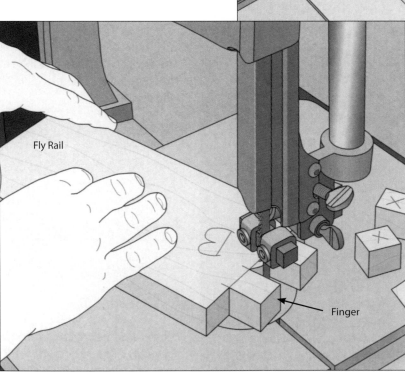

Fly Rail

Finger

2 Sawing the fingers. To cut the fingers at the end of the fly rail on your band saw, start by sawing out the waste at both edges of the piece with two intersecting cuts. To clear the waste between the fingers, nibble at it with the blade, pivoting the piece as necessary to avoid cutting into the fingers (left). Once all the fingers are cut, test-fit the joint and make any necessary adjustments with a chisel.

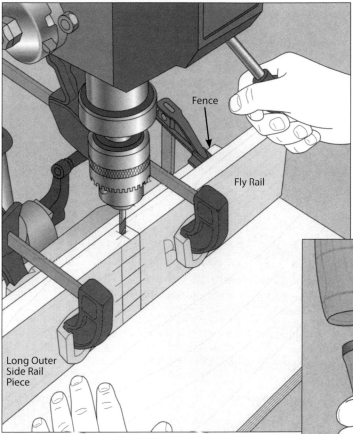

Fence

Fly Rail

Long Outer
Side Rail
Piece

3 Drilling the pin holes. Assemble each of the knuckle joints, then mark the center of the fingers on the top edge of the long rail piece. Bore the hole for the wooden pin on your drill press. Install a ¼-inch bit in the machine and clamp a backup panel to the table. Set the boards on the panel, aligning the center mark directly under the bit. Clamp a board against the back face of the stock, then secure it to the backup panel as a fence. Drill right through the stock (left). If the bit is not long enough to penetrate to the other edge of the boards, turn the stock over and complete the hole from the other side.

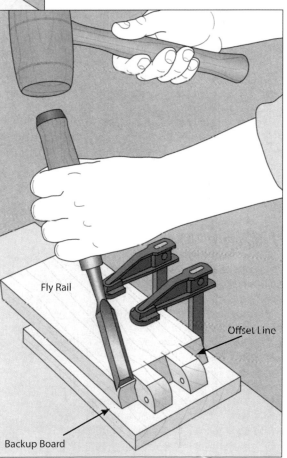

Fly Rail

Offset Line

Backup Board

4 Fine-tuning the knuckle joints. If the shoulders and fingers of the knuckle joints were left square, the fly rails would bind against the side rails when they were extended. To permit the joints to pivot, mark a line on the inside face of each fly rail and side rail piece parallel to the shoulder line and offset ½ inch from it. Clamp one fly rail inside-face up on a work surface with a backup board between the rail and the table. Start by using a chisel the same width as the fingers and notches to round over the end of the fingers. Then position the tip of the chisel blade on the offset line, centered on a notch, angling the tool so the cut will end at the original shoulder line. Holding the chisel with one hand, tap it with a wooden mallet to bevel the shoulder. Repeat for the remaining notches (right). Bevel the notches the same way on the long rail piece, but leave the fingers square.

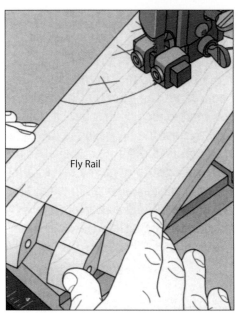

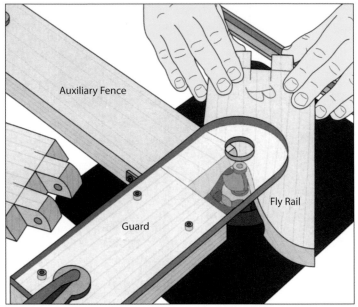

5 Cutting the fly rails to length.
Refer to the anatomy illustration (page 24) to mark the S-shaped cutting line on the fly rails, then designate the waste with Xs. Feed the stock across the band saw table (above), making certain neither hand is in line with the blade. Make matching cuts on the mating ends of the short outer rail pieces, ensuring that there will be a sufficiently large gap—about ½ inch—between the two boards for a handhold.

6 Routing finger recesses in the fly rails. To facilitate pivoting the fly rails, cut finger recesses into the underside of their curved ends. Install a piloted cove bit in a router, mount the tool in a table, and set the cutting depth at ⅝ inch. To provide a bearing surface for the rails, fashion a fence for the stock to ride against on the infeed side of the table and a guard for the bit from a ply-wood block and clear acrylic. Attach the guard and fence together and clamp them to the table. Press the stock against the pilot bearing as you feed each rail across the table (above); make the recess about 4 inches long and center it on the rail's curved end.

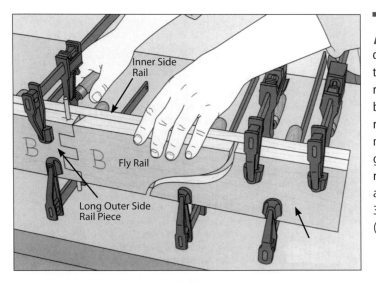

7 Gluing up the side rails. Assemble the knuckle joints, inserting lengths of ¼-inch dowel into the holes through the fingers, and cut the inner side rail pieces to length. For each side rail, spread glue on the contacting surfaces of the boards and clamp the outer rail pieces to the inner rail; do not apply any glue on the fly rail since it must be free to pivot. Make sure to leave a ½-inch gap between the fly rail and the short outer side rail piece. Alternate the clamps across the top and bottom edges of the assembly, spacing them 3 to 4 inches apart. Tighten the clamps evenly (right) until adhesive squeezes out of the joints.

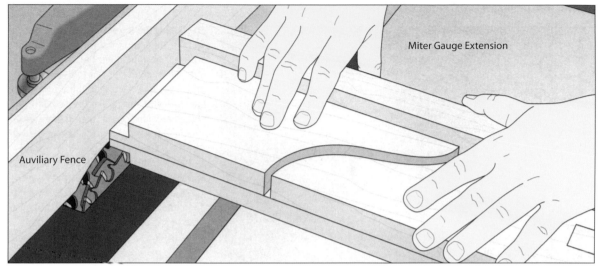

Miter Gauge Extension

Auxiliary Fence

8 Cutting the rail tenons. The next step in making the rails is to cut the tenons that will fit into the leg mortises. Start by drilling a test mortise (page 37), then outline the tenons on the ends of the rails, using the test mortise as a guide. Cut the tenons on your table saw fitted with a dado head; adjust the width of the head to slightly more than the tenon length—about ¾ inch. Set the cutting height at one-third the stock thickness. Attach an auxiliary fence to the saw's rip fence and an extension board to the miter gauge. To position the fence, align the shoulder line on the rail with the dado head and butt the fence against the end of the board. Feed the rail face down, holding the stock flush against the fence and the miter gauge extension. Turn the rail over and repeat the cut on the other side (above), fitting the tenon in the test mortise and raising the blades until the fit is snug. Cut tenon cheeks at the other end and repeat for each side and end rail. Next, flip the rail on edge and adjust the blade height to trim the tenons to width. Again, test the tenon until it fits snugly in the trial mortise.

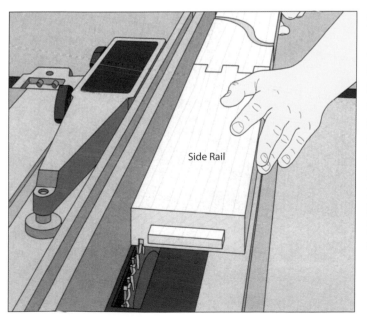

Side Rail

9 Preparing the rails for the top. Once all the tenons are finished, you will need to cut a groove along the inside face of the rails to accommodate the wood buttons that will secure the tabletop in place. Leave the dado head on your table saw, adjust its width to ¼ inch, and set the cutting height at about ⅞ inch. Position the fence about ¾ inch from the blades. Feed the rails into the dado head inside-face down and with the top edge pressed against the fence (left). Also cut a groove in the end rail blank at this time. This will ensure that all the grooves are identical. **(Caution: Blade guard removed for clarity.)**

Preparing the Drawer Rails and End Rail

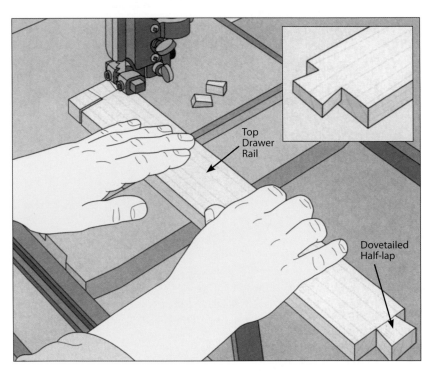

1 Cutting the top drawer rail. Cut the top drawer rail to length, then outline the dovetailed half-laps that will join the ends of the rail to the front legs of the table. Offset the outline toward the back edge of the rail so the dovetail will be centered on the leg when the rail's back edge is flush with the back face of the leg (step 2). Cut out the dovetails on your band saw, making two intersecting cuts along each edge of the outlines (left). Then use your table saw fitted with a dado head to cut away one-half the thickness of the dovetails from their bottom face (inset).

Top Drawer Rail

Dovetailed Half-lap

2 Cutting the dovetail sockets in the legs. Secure a front leg upright in a bench vise and use one of the dovetailed half-laps you cut in step 1 to outline the mating socket on the leg's top end. Make sure the top end of the leg is flush with the benchtop; this will support the router base plate as you cut the socket. Also ensure that the dovetail shoulder is butted against the inside edge of the leg and the rail's back edge is flush with the back face of the leg as you mark the lines. Install a ⅛-inch upcut-spiral straight bit into a router and adjust the cutting depth to the thickness of the dovetail. Rout the socket within the marked outline, then square the corners and pare to the line with straight and skew chisels, as needed. Repeat to cut the socket in the other front leg (right).

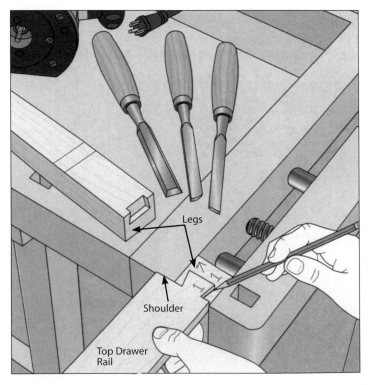

Legs

Shoulder

Top Drawer Rail

3 Cutting twin tenons in the bottom drawer rail.

The bottom drawer rail is joined to the legs with twin mortise-and-tenon joints. Cut the tenons at the ends of the rail on your table saw. Install a dado head ¾ inch wide, then set up a tenoning jig in the miter slot. Mark a twin tenon at each end of the rail and set the cutting height at ¾ inch. Lay out the tenons so the back edges of the rail and leg will align (step 4). Clamp the rail end-up in the jig, placing a shim between the two to prevent the dado head from contacting the jig. Shift the jig sideways to align one of the tenon marks with the dado head. To make the cut, push the jig forward, feeding the stock into the blades. Shift the jig to line up the dado head with the waste adjoining the twin tenons, making several passes until you have cleared away the excess wood (right). Repeat the cut at the other end of the rail.

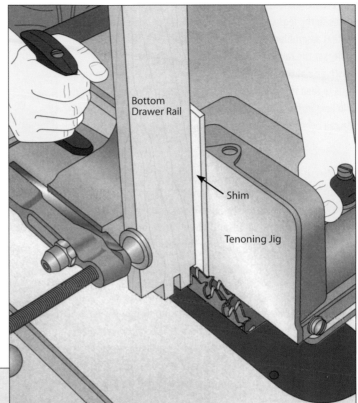

Bottom Drawer Rail

Shim

Tenoning Jig

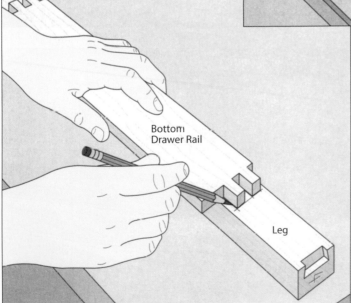

Bottom Drawer Rail

Leg

4 Outlining the double mortises in the legs.

Set one of the legs inside-face up on a work surface, then place the bottom drawer rail on it, aligning the back edge of the rail with the leg's back face. With the end of the rail at the appropriate height on the leg, outline the twin tenons with a pencil (left). Prepare the end rail (page 36) and drill out the rail mortises in the legs (page 37) before chiseling the double mortises in the legs (page 38).

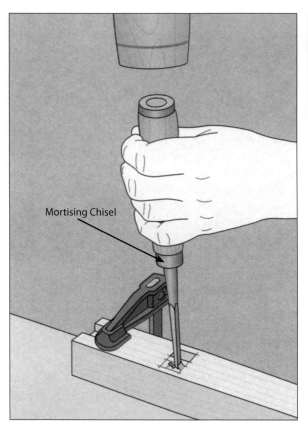

Mortising Chisel

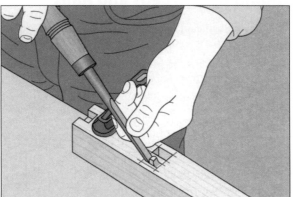

3 Chiseling the double mortises for the bottom drawer rail. Clamp a leg inside-face up to a work surface. Then, starting at one end of the double mortise outline, hold a mortising chisel square to the inside face of the leg and strike the handle with a wooden mallet (left). Use a chisel the same width as the mortises and be sure that the beveled side is facing the waste. Continue making cuts at intervals of about ⅛ inch until you reach the other end of the outline. Use the chisel to lever out the waste to the required depth (above). Chop out the remaining double mortises the same way. Test-fit the joints and widen or deepen the mortises with the chisel, as required.

4 Gluing the legs to the side rails. Test-assemble the legs and side rails, fine-tuning any ill-fitting joints with a chisel, if necessary. Sand any surfaces that will be difficult to access once the table is assembled. Next, spread glue on the contacting surfaces between one of the side rails and its corresponding legs, then fit the joints together, tapping them into final position with a wooden mallet, if required. Use two bar clamps to secure the joints. Aligning the bars with the side rail, lay the assembly on its side on a work surface with one clamp under the rail and one on top. Prop the tapered portion of the legs on wood blocks to keep the assembly level. Protecting the stock with wood pads, tighten the clamps evenly until a thin glue bead squeezes out of the joints (right). Repeat for the remaining side rail and legs.

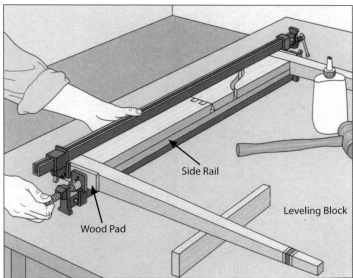

Side Rail

Leveling Block

Wood Pad

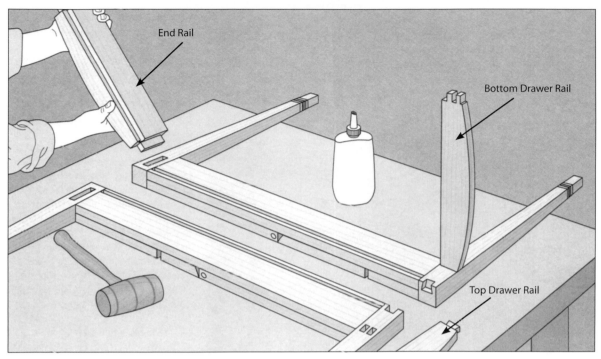

End Rail

Bottom Drawer Rail

Top Drawer Rail

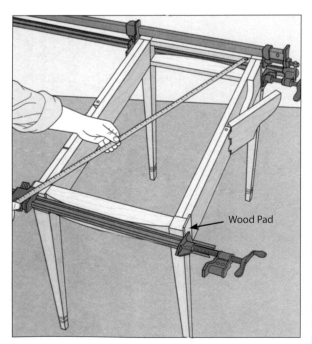

Wood Pad

5 **Gluing the end rail and drawer rails** Once the glue bonding the legs to the side rails has cured, remove the clamps and set the assemblies flat on a work surface with their mortises facing up. Test-fit and, if necessary, correct any ill-fitting joints and do any required sanding. Spread glue on the contacting surfaces between the end and drawer rails and the legs, then fit the bottom drawer rail and end rail into one of the side rail assemblies (above). Position the other leg-and-rail assembly on top and set the framework upright on the floor. Finally, fit the top drawer rail into place and clamp the assembly (step 6).

6 **Installing the clamps.** Use three bar clamps to secure the joints between the end and drawer rails and the legs. Protecting the stock with wood pads, install one clamp along the end rail and two more along the drawer rails. To check whether the assembly is square, measure the diagonals between opposite corners immediately after tightening the clamps (left). They should be equal; if not, the assembly is out-of-square. To correct the problem, install a bar clamp across the longer of the two diagonals. Tighten this clamp a little at a time, measuring as you go until the two diagonals are equal.

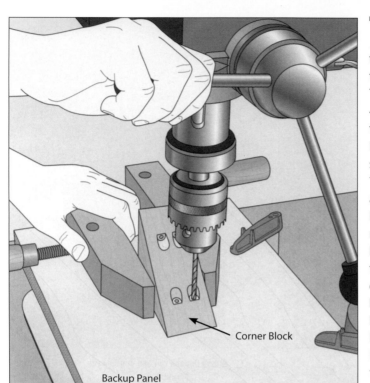

Backup Panel

Corner Block

7 **Making the corner blocks.** Attach a triangular corner block to each joint between the end rail and the side rails; this will reinforce the back corners of the table and keep it square. To fit the blocks into the table corners, make a 45° miter cut at each end of the blocks and mark four points on the long edge, two near each end. Next, bore pocket holes through the blocks for the screws that will secure them to the rails. Install a ½-inch Forstner bit in your drill press and clamp a backup panel to the machine table. Secure the block in a handscrew and drill a shallow hole to recess the screw head. Reposition the block to bore the next hole, then turn the block around in the handscrew to drill the holes near the other end. Repeat the process with a smaller brad-point bit to bore clearance holes (left). Finally, with the block top-face down on the table, drill a counter-bored hole through the middle of the surface; this hole will enable you to fasten to the block to the table top.

8 **Installing the corner blocks.** Spread glue on the contacting surfaces between the first block and the rails, hold the block in position against the rails and screw it in place. Repeat for the second block (right).

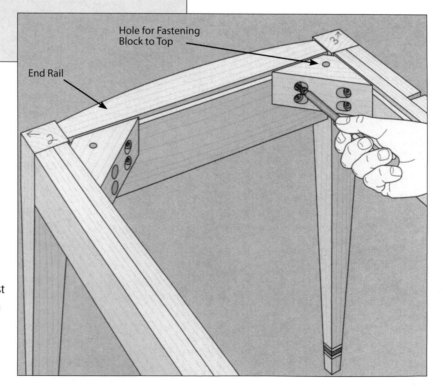

Hole for Fastening Block to Top

End Rail

Making the Drawer

Build the drawer for your Pembroke table as you would for a Queen Anne secretary, (page 116) using through dovetails to join the pieces. Use ¼-inch plywood for the drawer bottom. The Pembroke table drawer also gets a false front which is curved to match the shape of the end rail and drawer rails.

To install the drawer, start by fastening runners to the side rails, as shown below. Slide the drawer into its opening and clamp on the false front, then trace the curve of the top drawer rail onto the top edge of the false front (page 42) and cut the profile of the front. You can apply wax to the runners to help the drawer ride smoothly as it is opened and closed.

Supported by runners fastened to the side rails, the Pembroke table drawer shown above is assembled with through dovetails. The false front curves to match the profile of the end rail and drawer rails.

Reinforcing the Frame

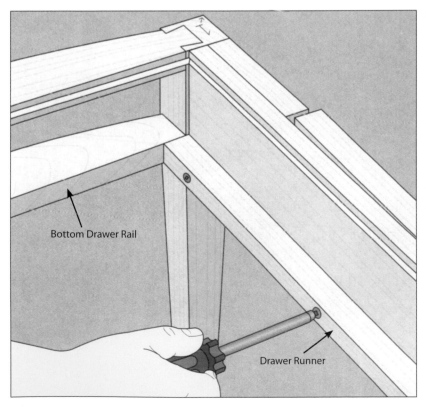

Bottom Drawer Rail

Drawer Runner

1 Installing the drawer runners. Size the drawer runners, cutting them a few inches longer than the drawer. Drill three holes through the edges of each one, locating one hole near each end and one at the middle. Holding an edge of the runner against the side rail and one end against the bottom drawer rail, screw it in place (left). The top face of the runner should be flush with the top face of the bottom drawer rail.

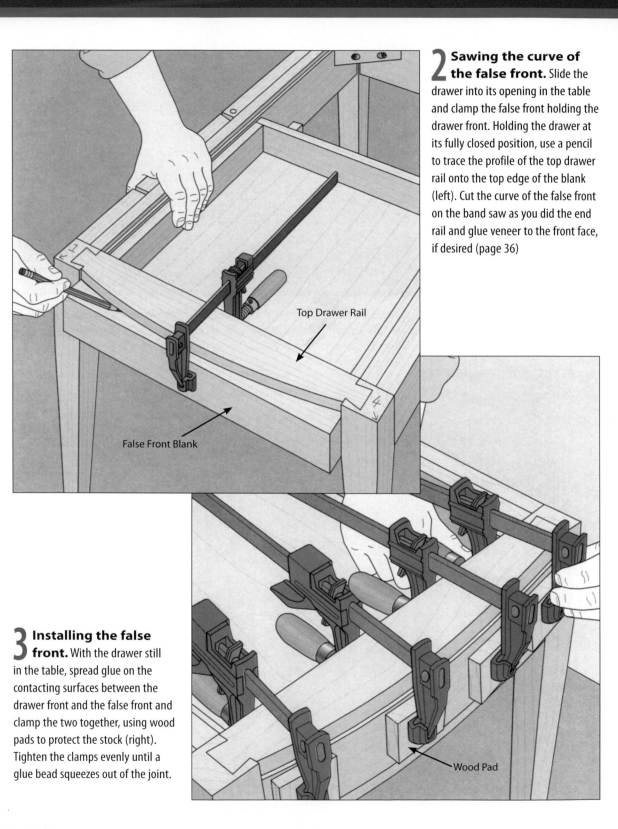

2 **Sawing the curve of the false front.** Slide the drawer into its opening in the table and clamp the false front holding the drawer front. Holding the drawer at its fully closed position, use a pencil to trace the profile of the top drawer rail onto the top edge of the blank (left). Cut the curve of the false front on the band saw as you did the end rail and glue veneer to the front face, if desired (page 36)

Top Drawer Rail

False Front Blank

3 **Installing the false front.** With the drawer still in the table, spread glue on the contacting surfaces between the drawer front and the false front and clamp the two together, using wood pads to protect the stock (right). Tighten the clamps evenly until a glue bead squeezes out of the joint.

Wood Pad

Making the Top

With the sides down, the top of the Pembroke table appears to be circular. Once the leaves are raised, however, the top's distinctive shape, with elliptical ends and sides, becomes apparent. Similar-shaped tabletops were used on Federal-period card tables. The leaves are hinged on a rule joint, which is shaped on the router table. Once the joint is completed and the hinges located, the curved profile of the leaves is cut on the band saw.

Shaping the Top

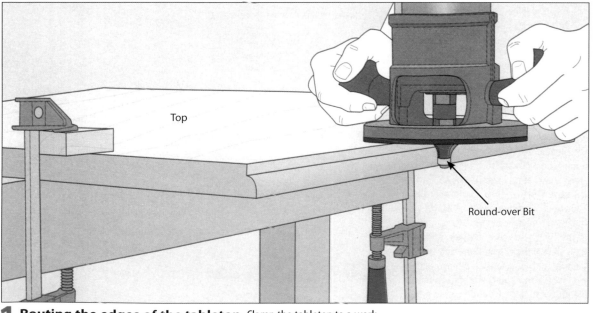

Top

Round-over Bit

1 **Routing the edges of the tabletop.** Clamp the tabletop to a work surface with the edge to be shaped extending off the surface. Install a piloted round-over bit and adjust the cutting depth to allow you to reach the final depth in at least two passes. As you make the cut, press the bit pilot against the stock throughout the pass (above). For a smooth finish, make your final pass a slow and shallow one.

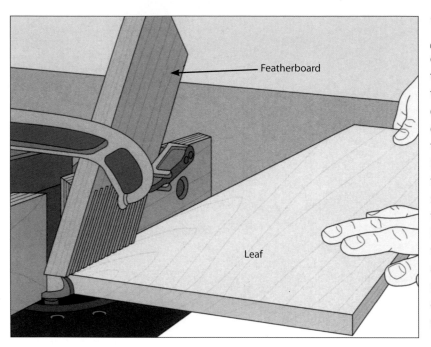

Featherboard

Leaf

2 Routing the cove in the leaves. Install a piloted cove bit in the router and mount the tool in a table. Align the fence with the bit pilot bearing so the width of cut will equal one-half the cutter diameter. Clamp a featherboard to the fence on the infeed side of the bit to hold the workpiece flat against the router table. Set the depth of cut shallow to start; make several passes to reach your final depth gradually. Feed the leaf into the bit, pressing the edge of the workpiece firmly against the fence (left). After each pass, test-fit the pieces until the top and the leaf mesh with a very slight gap between the two.

3 Attaching the leaves to the top. Join the leaves to the top by installing rule-joint hinges on the underside of the pieces. Set the top and leaves face down on a work surface, then mark lines along the shaped edges of the top in line with the start of each round-over cut, known as the fillet (inset). Install three hinges for each leaf: one in the middle of the joint and one 5 inches from each end. With a paper shim inserted between the leaf and top, position a hinge leaf against the top and the other against the leaf at each hinge location so the pin is aligned with the fillet line, then outline the hinge. Chisel out the mortises, using a wider-blade tool to cut the mortises for hinge leaves and a narrower chisel to cut the slots for the pins (right). Screw the hinges in place.

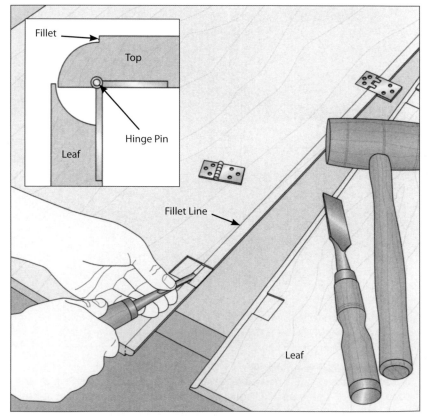

Fillet

Top

Hinge Pin

Leaf

Fillet Line

Leaf

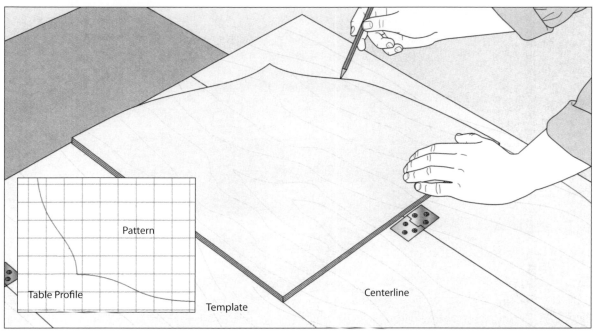

Pattern

Table Profile

Template

Centerline

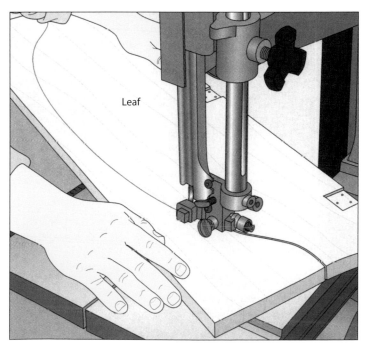

Leaf

4 Outlining the profile of the top.
Enlarge the grid shown in the inset to produce a cutting pattern for shaping the profile of the top; one square equals 2 inches. Trace the pattern onto a piece of ¼-inch plywood or hardboard and cut out the template on your band saw. Then set the top face-down on a work surface and extend the leaves. Mark a line down the middle of the top and position the template on it; align the straight edge of the pattern with the centerline and the adjoining curved edge with the end of the top. Use a pencil to trace the curved profile on the top. Repeat at the remaining corners (above).

5 Cutting the profile of the top.
Unscrew the leaves from the top and use your band saw to cut the curved profile into each of the three pieces. Cut just to the waste side of your cutting line (left), feeding the stock with both hands and keeping your fingers clear of the blade. Sand the cut edges to the line.

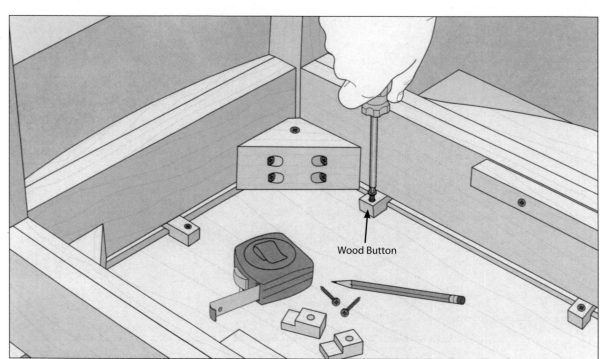

Wood Button

Shop Tip

Using steel tabletop fasteners

Commercial steel tabletop fasteners work like wood buttons: They are screwed to the top from underneath and grip a groove cut along the inside face of the rails. Because commercial fasteners are thinner than lipped wood buttons, the groove does not have to be cut with a dado blade (page 33); you can use a standard saw blade or a three-wing slotting cutter in a table-mounted router. To ensure proper tension, make the groove a little farther from the top than you would with the wood buttons.

6 Installing the top. The top is fastened to the table rails with wood buttons; screwed to the top, the buttons feature lips that fit into grooves cut into the rails (page 33), providing a secure connection while allowing for wood movement. Reinstall the rule-joint hinges in the top and leaves, and place the top face down on a work surface. Make a button for every 6 inches of rail length (page 133). Spacing them about 6 inches apart and leaving a ½-inch gap between the bottom of the grooves and the lipped ends of the buttons, screw the buttons in place (above). Once all the buttons are attached, drive a screw through each corner block into the top.

POCKET-HOLE JIG

You can use pocket holes with screws as an alternative to wood buttons for attaching a tabletop to the side and end rails. The holes are drilled at an angle, and a pocket-hole jig (left, top), shop-built from ¾-inch plywood, makes simple work of boring the holes on your drill press. For the jig, screw the two sides of the cradle together to form an L. Then cut a 90° wedge from each support bracket so that the wide side of the cradle will sit at an angle of about 15° from the vertical. Screw the brackets to the jig base and glue the cradle to the brackets.

To use the jig, seat a rail in the cradle with the side that will be drilled facing up. Drill the holes in two steps with two different bits: Use a Forstner bit twice the diameter of the screw heads for the entrance holes and a brad-point bit slightly larger than the diameter of the screw shanks for the exit holes. (The larger brad-point bit allows for wood expansion and contraction.)

To begin the process, install the brad-point bit and, with the drill press off, lower the bit with the feed lever, then position the jig and workpiece to center the bottom edge of the workpiece on the bit (inset). Clamp the jig to the table and replace the brad-point bit with the Forstner bit.

Feed the bit slowly to drill the holes just deep enough to recess the screw heads. Then, install the brad-point bit and bore through the workpiece to complete the pocket holes (left, bottom).

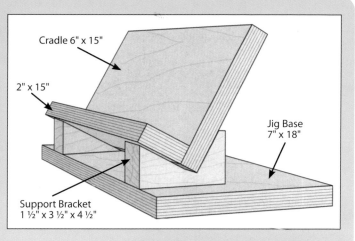

Cradle 6" x 15"

2" x 15"

Jig Base
7" x 18"

Support Bracket
1 ½" x 3 ½" x 4 ½"

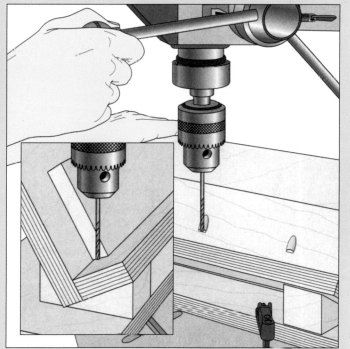

Index

More Great Books from Fox Chapel Publishing

Back to *Basics*
Straight Talk for Today's Woodworker

Get *Back to Basics* with the core information you need to succeed.

Cabinet Construction
ISBN: 978-1-56523-529-8
$19.95 • 144 Pages

Woodworker's Guide to Turning
ISBN: 978-1-56523-498-7
$19.95 • 144 Pages

Fundamentals of Sharpening
ISBN: 978-1-56523-496-3
$19.95 • 120 Pages

Woodworker's Guide to Carving
ISBN: 978-1-56523-497-0
$19.95 • 160 Pages

Setting Up Your Workshop
ISBN: 978-1-56523-463-5
$19.95 • 152 Pages

Woodworking Machines
ISBN: 978-1-56523-465-9
$19.95 • 192 Pages

Woodworker's Guide to Wood
ISBN: 978-1-56523-464-2
$19.95 • 160 Pages

Constructing Kitchen Cabinets
ISBN: 978-1-56523-466-6
$19.95 • 144 Pages

Woodworker's Guide to Joinery
ISBN: 978-1-56523-462-8
$19.95 • 192 Pages

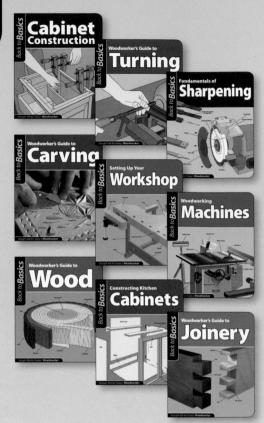

BUILT to LAST

Discover the timeless projects in the *Built to Last Series.* These are the projects that stand the test of time in function and form, in the techniques they employ, and represent the pieces every woodworker should build in a lifetime.

Shaker Furniture
12 Timeless Woodworking Projects
By Editors of Skills Institute Press
Step-by-step projects for building beautiful Shaker furniture for every room of the house.

ISBN: 978-1-56523-467-3
$19.95 • 144 Pages

Outdoor Furniture
14 Timeless Woodworking Projects for the Yard, Deck, and Patio
By Editors of Skills Institute Press
Design and build beautiful wooden outdoor furniture sturdy enough to withstand Mother Nature with the detailed techniques and step by step instructions in this handy guide.

ISBN: 978-1-56523-500-7
$19.95 • 144 Pages

Look for These Books at Your Local Bookstore or Woodworking Retailer

To order direct, call **800-457-9112** or visit *www.FoxChapelPublishing.com*

By mail, please send check or money order + S&H to:
Fox Chapel Publishing, 1970 Broad Street, East Petersburg, PA 17520

# Item	Shipping Rate	
1 Item	$3.99 US	$8.98 CAN
Each Additional	.99 US	$3.99 CAN

International Orders - please email info@foxchapelpublishing.com or visit our website for actual shipping costs.